C000230355

Ireland's Whiskey Guide

by **Kate Amber**

Amber Publishers

About me

My life is a bit like a voyage on a sailing boat. I'm happy to sail along and enjoy my journey; the myriad of meetings, adventures and experiences. My positive attitude and humour have always been my constant companions! According to my life motto 'in every problem, there's a clue to the solution', or so I believe. Until now life has steered me from one harbour to the next, staying a short time in one and sometimes longer in another. Some I deliberately stayed in for a while, others I found myself in by chance. Now I have finally laid anchor in Ireland where I'm living out one of my childhood dreams, which is capturing the beauty of this land with my camera. The history of Ireland, the country and its people have awoken within me a desire to write this book.

Ireland's Whiskey Guide
Autor: Kate Amber
ISBN 978-1-5272-3733-9
Paperback Edition
Published by Amber Publishers, Dublin, Ireland,
www.amberpublishers.com
+353 86400 7460
First Edition

Disclaimer

visit **www.irelandswhiskeyguide.com**

Contents

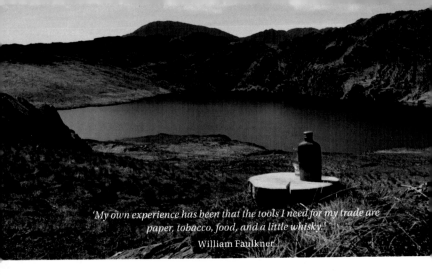

Foreword

Up to two years ago, I would never have guessed, that I, of all people, would write a book about whiskey. I was convinced that whiskey and liquor in general were just not for me. My first encounter with the 'liquid gold' was totally accidental. I was collecting friends from Dublin airport and on our way to Galway we stopped for a break. By chance we ended up in Kilbeggan Whiskey Distillery. From then on, the old craft of whiskey making and its history became a passion of mine; tasting and sampling included of course!

... and now here we are, three years later and this book has somehow written itself! I invite you on a journey through the colourful history of whiskey in Ireland. A wee word of caution, as this tale will take you through grisly tales of destruction and plundering of monasteries during the time of Henry VIII. Read why the introduction of taxes in 1661 allowed Ireland to become a whiskey empire in the 19th century and – mysteriously enough – what role angels play in all of this.

In this book you will discover that Ireland was not only a world champion in whiskey distilling, but also in producing and smuggling illegally distilled alcohol. The Americans lovingly call it moonshine and the Irish 'poitín'.

All in all, we are talking about the secrets and mysteries of illegally distilled alcohol. You will read unbelievable stories about hidden distilleries, like where one distillery was built into a cliff face and only discovered when a storm flood flushed it out! Journey with me as we explore the intricacies of how Irish whiskey briefly lost its prime position, but is now back on its way to success and its old fame. I invite you to come on a journey of discovery. Follow me as the history of Irish whiskey is being re-written. Why re-written you ask? We will come to that later.

Although I have intensively researched the history of the manufacturing of whiskey in Ireland over the course of the last year, I am very aware that I cannot show you all the ins and outs of this craft. While I was working on this book, the world of Irish whiskey was changing so fast, that I not only had to change the whole focus of the book, but also had to add new places and new tours. Of course the development itself is not finished, just because the book is. Almost every day it seems a new distillery opens and I hope that you become 'thirsty' enough to come to Ireland and immerse yourself in the world of Irish whiskey.

Perhaps you ask yourself: 'Why should Ireland be the perfect place for the liquid gold?' It is just a little bigger than Bavaria, a bit cold, a little wet and definitely windy. I am sure you will find the answers to these questions within these pages.

With this guide, you will receive a taste of different whiskey types, insight into the magic of making whiskey and an in-depth view into some very special places. During my travels, I had the company of Shem, my native driver and Irish expert, so you will get the story from two different points of view. Many times, his Irish ways were the key to people opening up and chatting with us. A big thank you to Shem for driving me through this beautiful country. It goes without saying that it was very useful to have a driver as without one I would not have been able to sensitise my taste buds so thoroughly to the high quality of Irish whiskey! *Sláinte!*

'There is no such thing as a bad whisky.
Some whiskies just happen to be better than others.'
William Faulkner

The history of whiskey –
a thousand years of tradition

The ongoing argument between the Irish and the Scots as to who discovered whiskey first is nearly as old as whiskey itself. Personally, I'm inclined to think that the production of the 'Liquid Gold' is likely to have begun around the same time in both countries.

THE BEGINNINGS

In the 5th century AD, Christian Monks began to convert the Celts to Christianity. The monks had, beside their ironclad religious beliefs, also vast knowledge of techniques for distilling medicines and perfumes. The monasteries at this time were the focus for classical education acting as nascent universities. Irish (Gaeilge) is a Celtic language related to languages spoken in Scotland and parts of Wales and France, so when the monks visited these places, they could easily exchange and gather knowledge.

COLUMBANUS – AN IRISH MONK'S JOURNEY THROUGH EUROPE

Between the 6th and 8th centuries, there flourished in Ireland and Scotland a distinct Celtic Church, relatively independent of Rome, which undertook mission work across Europe, sending out Irish monks to reignite the flame of Christianity during the so-called Dark Ages in Europe.

According to legend, an Irish monk Columbanus (the Dove) and several companions, including St. Gallus, journeyed across Europe all the way down to Lake Constance and Switzerland. Although these monks were on a holy mission to convert and spread Christianity throughout Europe, they ended up leaving a legacy of their own. Gallus ended up establishing the city of St. Gallen while Columbanus continued his journey from Luxeuil into Italy where he founded the Monastery of Bobbio.

Regarding the little-known secrets of the history of whiskey and spirits throughout time, there is an intriguing connection between the ancient Egyptians and these monks. The Egyptians used a distillation method for making perfumes which also created the basis for alcohol distillation. The monks further refined this process and used this high percent alcohol as a medical solution with the inclusion of herbs and natural remedies. The use of spirits came into its own at this time when hygiene was not of paramount concern, so the monks used this 'medicinal alcohol' as a disinfectant and for wound cleaning. The effective use of medicinal alcohol both internally for stomach illnesses and as an external disinfectant soon became a health craze. No wonder the liquid was soon dubbed the 'Water of Life' – a phrase that's still making the rounds today, depending which pub you go to.

Christian monastic settlement, Glendalough, Co. Wicklow

The etymology of the word 'whiskey' comes from the Irish language (Gaeilge). In Scotland it was called 'uisgebeath' and in Ireland 'uiscebeatha' both meaning the 'water of life', however, for non-Gaelic speakers, the pronunciation is not without its difficulties, therefore the soldiers of King Henry II who conquered Ireland in 1171, commandeered the word and mangled it into something like 'fuiscee', which over the course of time, became 'whiskey'.

In Ireland by the way, whiskey is still seen as a 'one size fits all' type of cure. It doesn't matter if you have a cold, or a tummy bug, if a baby is teething or for any other pain – mental, broken heart or physical – whiskey will cure you, of this as I have been reassured repeatedly.

When treating patients in pain, the monks quickly realised that the digestion of this alcoholic liquid caused them to be in 'great spirits', an English phrase describing a good mood – no surprise there! Perhaps this is the reason why alcohol is now called 'spirits'.

Thanks to old tax documentation from 1494, we know that scottish monks had to pay tax on the sale of whiskey (from barley). This doesn't mean they were the first to manufacture it, just that they were already paying tax on it. In the 'Red Book of the Diocese of Ossory' (near Kilkenny in Ireland), Bishop de Ledrede had already put down on paper in the 13th century, how 'aqua vitae' was produced. So these facts confirm that whiskey, with its magical healing properties, was being produced in both countries from an early stage.

Clonmacnoise Monastic Site, Shannonbridge

THE GOLDEN PERIOD OF IRISH WHISKEY

Mid 16th century, the then King of England, ridden with financial troubles set out to plunder all the Catholic monasteries in England, Ireland and Wales between 1536 and 1541. The monks lost the majority of their wealth, their homes and their livelihood. To survive, they blended into the communities and sold the little they had left: their knowledge.

Boyle Abbey, Boyle

In addition to serving God, the pursuit of knowledge and learning were encouraged as monastic work. The monks proved useful in the community, not just for their ability to read and write, but in their knowledge of the craft of distilling spirits and whiskey.

For the Emerald Isle, this age became a golden era for whiskey distillation and also 'poitín', the illegal, not so well-known brother of whiskey. There quickly developed two separate business branches: the official business of small and large whiskey distilleries and also, the unofficial distillation of poitín.

Poitín

We are talking about the 16th century, when there was no electricity or delivery service, therefore almost every little village was self sufficient with its own shop with basic needs, a church, a pub, a mill and a small distillery. The village life was shaped by social cohesion, that's why people would meet in the house with the biggest kitchen. Food and drink were either brought or bought there, and that's how they spent their time together. Singers and story tellers also visited the villages and entertained in the evenings. Moreover, the death watches took place right there as well.

The distillation of alcohol was neither as developed nor as safe as it is nowadays. Because of the poisonous gases that were not extracted from the alcohol, it could happen that people fell into a coma and it could take up to 7 days before they awoke from it. So, if somebody died, he or she was laid out in a coffin which would have been put onto a table in the middle of the room. For three days his family and friends would hold vigil by the body to check in case he might

Slane Distillery, Slane, Co. Meath

wake up again. During this time the villagers would chat, eat, sing and dance and of course also drink together. This tradition is maintained until this day and is called a 'wake'. After 3 days the person was buried, but to be sure that he was not in a 7-day coma, a string was put on his hand which was connected to a bell on the surface of his grave. After the funeral, it was the responsibility of the grave yard employees to listen out for the bell ringing. It is from this time period that phrases like 'buried alive', 'raised from the dead' and 'saved by the bell' originate.

The history of poitín making has very little evidence in written documentation. Just about everybody – other than the revenue man – would likely have been in on the secret of where a bottle might be obtained, but as this was something passed along by word of mouth – a friend of a friend, we can only surmise that it was made and in huge quantities, all of which avoided the heavy taxes imposed on whiskey. Any documentation there is, will be found only in court records. The popular defense was to plead that, 'it's medicine for my cattle, your Honour'.

In recent times, the revenue decided they'd be better off allowing poitín to be distilled legally as this would then give them additional revenue. That being said, I have no doubt that a friend of a friend could very likely acquire a tax-free bottle from a secret source.

It's not surprising that because of all the secrecy involved, until only a few years ago, it was a punishable offence to manufacture and possess poitín. Although poitín was produced anywhere you could hide a still, court records found in Donegal show that there were distilleries hidden in the mountains or even on the craggy cliffs of the coast. One infamous distillery, hidden on the side of a cliff, was only discovered due to damaging floods. In recent times archaeologists have uncovered more hidden distilleries in coastal cliff areas where fully functioning stills existed.

Stills were often relocated overnight with the aim of making life difficult for the excise man while continuing to maintain supply to customers. For stills closer to civilisation, it was common practice to use rotting turnips to mask the smells from distilling – and keep the revenue at bay.

From old police records from Great Britain, we can see that the Irish produced lots of poitín, so much in fact that there was a special police task force sent to Donegal to handle it. The spirit was of such good quality that the Scots started importing it – obviously tax free. It goes without saying that an officer lucky enough to chance upon finding these stashes of poitín – or its drinkers – was in for a big pay day. Around this time the number of soldiers and tax hunters native to the area rose dramatically, due to their inside knowledge of who was doing what and where they were doing it.

WHISKEY

Unfortunately, there are not many reports from this golden era. The reason for this lies in the British occupation which lasted for 800 years and didn't really entertain the documentation of whiskey and poitín.

Interestingly enough, however, if you study any street map from that period, you will find a Distillery Street in almost every town and city. Today, there are various private organisations researching and investigating all the old distilleries and their names in order to catalogue their histories.

Due to our ever-present curiosity about the past, court records, revenue documents and even our whiskey connoisseur Alfred Barnard's book are being examined to help find any secrets that could illuminate its history. The project led by Deirdre Keon from 'Midlands Whiskey Experiences' in

Inside the Pub 'The Duke of York', Belfast

Athlone is the best example of this. During eight months of research she discovered that there had been three distilleries and 38 breweries in the town. Today there is very little to remind us of this time.

Soon we will discover just how tied to the past whiskey is in the Ireland of today. We'll do this through conversations in distilleries and pubs and

Tax Man Desk in Tullamore D.E.W. Old Bonded Warehouse

with older generations. We'll find out that there was a nationwide tradition of whiskey distillation. The point being that wherever there was a mill, there was usually a distillery beside it. You could say, 'Where there's a mill, there's a way.'

THE INVENTION OF THE 'PURE POT STILL WHISKEY'

In 17th century England, Charles II sat on the throne and the British crown suffered from a lack of funds, as it virtually always had – a problem present day governments still struggle with – however, the methods to fill the coffers were slightly different in those days. The Chancellor of the Exchequer was constantly on the lookout for new sources of income. It was widely known that the trade with illegally distilled alcohol was rampant and there was no taxation on this very lucrative market. The aim was to gain better control of the individual distilleries.

Taxes on every bottle of whiskey sold did not prevent the fact that barrels could be bought on the black market. While taxing the barrels, one could not be sure if all the potential revenue had been considered, therefore, the monarchy decided on the 24th of December 1661, to bring in a new tax on a special part of the production process. The ingredient barley malt which is used for the fermentation process was taxed, making it more difficult for distilleries to avoid paying tax, whether they actually sold their products or not. The British monarchy, however, underestimated the Irish trait of not taking life in general, and foreign laws in particular, too seriously and also the Irish talent for finding ways to bypass them. So before long, a solution to this tax problem was found – the so called 'work around'.

Up to this point barley malt traditionally had been used in the production of whiskey, however, through this implementation of the new tax, the Irish discovered a replacement mixture of barley malt and unprocessed barley. To this day, this mixture is described as 'Pure Pot Still Whiskey' although I would prefer 'Tax Avoidance Whiskey'. Whatever you want to call it, the year 1661 was the year a British king actively assisted in the birth of Irish whiskey. So, it does not matter who invented this golden liquid, what does matter though, is who was the first to produce pure pot still whiskey, because it's only this you can actually call 'Irish Whiskey'.

Here we have an example of a brilliant discovery. A situation where necessity is the mother of invention. In this case the necessity was tax avoidance. Since the distilleries did not want to pay the new tax, they were forced to think of a solution and that is how the Irish discovered a drink with a truly exceptional taste: Irish whiskey.

THE INTRODUCTION OF DISTILLATION RIGHTS

Approximately 100 years later, in 1779, the British Parliament decided to introduce a new measurement to enable a higher tax band for distilleries. This time the tax would be applied to an estimated product amount, and not to the actual – official – product amount as before.

As a result, the number of official distilleries shrank to as little as two in 1802. At the same time the number of 'unofficial' distilleries producing whiskey rose dramatically. This can be seen as a time of British prohibition. Ultimately the tax revenue dropped instead of rose, so that this tax law was repealed after 20 years.

Instead of the estimated amount of liquid, the

Photo of the old Jameson Distillery in Bow St., Dublin

actual amount produced was taxed, leaving producers at a loss. To make up for this financial setback, the Crown introduced a fee of ten pounds which had to be paid if a distillery wanted to acquire the distillation right. As a result most new distilleries were founded by the English, as the Irish simply did not have enough money to pay the distillation right fee. In typical Irish fashion, they put up a fight to produce their 'uiscebeatha' (Irish for 'water of life'). The fight against the whiskey black market was, and still remains, a failed conquest. Neither the tax man – called 'gauges' – nor the high financial penalties could hinder the Irish from producing their whiskey at a more affordable price, even today.

A TURNING POINT IN THE WHISKEY PRODUCTION

Ireland is only a little bigger than Bavaria, but during the 19th century, 60% of the worldwide whiskey demand was produced in Ireland. This truly was and is a whiskey imperium. This is even more amazing when you con-

Whiskey Fire in Dublin, The Illustrated London News depicts the fire in the Liberties in 1875.
Photograph: Illustrated London News/ South Dublin County Council Digital Library

sider that the amount of poitín produced wasn't even factored into that.

As the demand for whiskey was incredibly high, new plans were needed to increase the production. This was finally achieved by the introduction of the 'Column Still' procedure, invented by Robert Stein and perfected to marketability by Irish man, Aeneas Coffey. You will learn more about this method and the differences to the traditional way in the chapter 'Whiskey Manufacturing Processes'. Unfortunately, this change meant the beginning of the end of the original pure pot whiskey and ultimately, also the end of the 'golden era' for Irish whiskey distilleries. From 1830 onwards, through the replacement of the pot still with the new column still, a new age in terms of whiskey production had begun.

The journalist Alfred Barnard was the author of the first book about whiskey, written in 1885/86. He travelled during a three year period throughout England, Ireland and Scotland and wrote about most of the whiskey distilleries he visited. The detailed guide his works produced laid

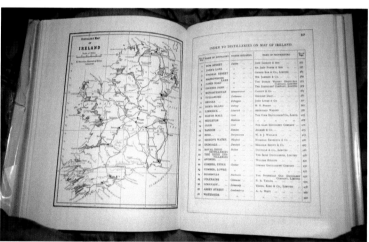

The Whisky Distilleries of the United Kingdom by Alfred Barnard

the foundation for research into whiskey's colourful past. Barnard could not have foreseen the impact his work would have almost 100 years later. As luck would have it, Alfred Barnard had visited Dublin before 1875 and captured the beauty and prosperity of the local whiskey distilleries.

In 1875, the Liberties' Whiskey Fire happened – the biggest disaster in Victorian Dublin. In a part of the city known as The Liberties, a few malt houses and adjoining warehouses caught fire. As a result, whiskey poured through the streets like burning lava, leaving a path of destruction through wide parts of the city. The firefighting operation was most difficult as the wind fanned the fire continuously and the panic of the people and animals that fled through the streets hindered the efforts of firefighters. As the fire was finally put out, the scene of destruction was terrible and many buildings were burned to the ground. The fire caused Dublin the greatest financial damage of the 19th century. Fortunately, it claimed only a handful of lives and while some died due to the alcoholic fumes, many of the deaths and injuries were caused, not by the fire, but by people collecting the burning liquid in glasses and pots, even in their own shoes and drinking it without caring that it contained all sorts of dirt and horse faeces from the street and the water used to put out the fire.

Irish whiskey advertising signs

Without Alfred Barnard's book we would know nothing about the beauty of the old buildings, the architectural finesse and the innovations that were coming into use in the old days of distilleries. Some sources state that in 1800, over 400 different Irish whiskey brands were known in America. These were made in the approximately 160 official Irish distilleries of that time. It was the peak time for the Irish whiskey industry. Especially popular were brands like Roe and Jameson, although there were plenty of smaller, less known distilleries, which only produced for the regional market. Powers and Paddy are prime examples of this, as well as distilleries that were specialised in the supply, like Locke's from Kilbeggan.

WHISKEY VS WHISKY - THE ATTEMPT OF A PURITY LAW

From 1860, the British Empire allowed two different processes of whiskey production to be mixed. Distilleries and traders began to combine the pot still with the less expensive column still to create a cheaper product For the Irish distillers, this was a catastrophe. Many of the traditional Irish producers said that such a mixture could simply not be called whiskey. The Scottish had no such qualms and were actually quite successful with the distribution of this new type of whiskey mix. When the sales dropped, the Irish distilleries in Dublin formed an allegiance: John Powers & Sons, John Jameson & Son and George Roe together would preserve their traditions. As a rebuke to these precarious changes they came together and published a book titled 'Truths about Whisky'. As you can see the word whisky is spelled without an 'e'. The idea was to attract public attention to the 'watered down' whiskey and the consequences to traditional Irish whiskey making.

The central aim for the Irish distilleries was the production of an especially high-quality whiskey. To achieve this, the distillers Powers, George Roy, Jameson and Bushmills went before a sort of tribunal with the rather long title of 'The Royal Commission on Whisky and Other Potable Spirits'. The goal of their legal action was to ensure that drink produced in the cheaper column still fashion could not be sold as 'whiskey'. The

Advertising for Georg Roe Whiskey

Scottish got wind of this and acted quickly. Some distilleries started to call their products 'Whisky' - omitting the 'e'. Unfortunately, the Irish distillers did not win their legal suite and in 1909 the case was dismissed. All the same, the original group of plaintiffs remained true to their traditional Irish pot still, but of course it was more expensive. You will find the explanation for this and the roll the tax inspector Coffey played in all this in more detail in the chapter 'Manufacturing of Whiskey'.

PROHIBITION AND TWO WORLD WARS

In 1922, Ireland at long last became independent of Great Britain, a goal that the Irish people had been dreaming of and fighting for over 800 years. Unfortunately, the British 'punished' the Irish for their successful quest for independence with a trade embargo, which brought the whiskey production almost to a standstill. Additionally, in 1919, prohibition swept through the United States and as Ireland's main whiskey income was from the USA, it was hit very hard by these limitations. Whiskey needs time to mature and as there was very little production for a period of 10 years, Ireland couldn't cover the US demand once prohibition had been lifted. Countries like Scotland had the advantage. Being part of the United Kingdom, they had constant access to the market in England and the British colonies. Their position in the international market was strengthened, particularly as most English owners of the Irish distilleries sold up and returned to the UK out of fear they would lose their investment. The outbreak of the Second World War also meant a halt in whiskey production. Resources were needed to feed the population. All of this resulted in the slow death of Irish whiskey production.

Of course whiskey was still sold on the black market during prohibition, often hidden in old whiskey bottles, which happened to be mostly Jameson bottles. Jameson would later suffer an image and reputation crisis from this bootleg drink being sold in their bottles. The damage to Jameson's reputation was enormous and it took the company decades to gain their clients' trust again in order to build the brand into the well-known drink it is today.

From 1930 onwards, most distilleries stopped production and by 1948 only four distilleries remained: Jameson, Powers, Bushmills and Paddy.

These were the only survivors of the hard times. To cement a stronger position in the market, three of these companies, Jameson, Powers and Paddy founded the 'Irish Distillers Group'.

D.W.D. Whiskey Distillery closed down around 1945

In 1975 the head office of this association moved to Midleton in County Cork, where a restructuring took place.

In 1980, the Irish government passed a law called the 'Irish Whiskey Act', which allowed the combination of malt whiskey and the low-priced method of the column still. Moreover, the caramel colorant E150 was permitted to be used so that this mix looked like the real whiskey. Traditionally, a product could only be labelled as Irish whiskey if the alcohol was stored in a wooden barrel for three years and a day and then, only in Ireland. So, if you like the idea of producing your own Irish whiskey, you need to purchase alcohol in a wooden barrel and store it for three years and at least 24 hours – anywhere, as long as it's in Ireland – otherwise you're out of luck and it won't be Irish whiskey.

THE HISTORICAL TRACES OF WHISKEY PRODUCTION IN TODAY'S IRELAND

As we've explored, whiskey manufacturing has very deep roots in Ireland

and the tradition, while overcoming a somewhat tumultuous struggle, has been making a steady comeback. For example, the beautiful village of Clonegal, located on the border of counties Carlow and Wexford and although it rhymes nicely with Donegal, it's nowhere near it. It is home to a castle which is open to the public during the summer months.

Ruins of Burt Distillery, Burt, County Donegal

From the descendants of the former owners who live there still, we learned many interesting things regarding the history of the family and the castle itself. We were told that in former times, a mill with a Simon Lacy distillery existed there. Unfortunately, a fire destroyed the mill and the buildings were never restored, however, we could still visit the ruins. An elderly lady from nearby explained to us that this place once had a colourful past with plenty of employment.

From these glamorous times the old pub Osborne's remains. Here it feels as if time has stood still. This pub has the title of being one of the oldest pubs in Ireland. And just like Clonegal, there are many sleepy little villages all over Ireland, that can look back to a history closely connected to the production of whiskey.

Ruins of Simon Lacy Distillery, Clonegal, Carlow,

The production of whiskey – the journey from barley to Irish gold

The following information is aimed mainly at novices or people who are not too familiar with this topic and those who would like to refresh their knowledge. For those who are already familiar with the production of whiskey – feel free to skip this chapter or stay curious and test yourself.

There are obvious steps that are identical in all manufacturing processes, but from a certain point onwards regional differences and procedures often based on historical differences come into play.

RAW MATERIALS

The chief ingredient for Irish whiskey has always been – and still is to this day – barley. Water and yeast are obviously important too. Interestingly enough in Scotland, corn was also used. Many Irish who had emigrated to the USA intended to produce whiskey in the same way as they had done back in Ireland. Unfortunately, they found that bar-

ley doesn't grow as abundantly as in Ireland. Whiskey in America took on a more Scottish tone and was also produced from corn. This made it distinct in itself.

The Malting

In the past, barley was washed in hot water to encourage the grains to sprout. Thereafter, the grain was spread over heated tiles and was moistened with water – it was like the barley had a spa day. The smoky taste of the Scottish whiskey derives from the turf that is used to heat the barley. As the grains absorbed all these different aromas, the Irish, in contrast to the Scottish, used odorless fuels. The temperature was held around 80 degrees for up to four days, so that the barley started the germination process. Because of this, the grains produced a certain starch, which was later required in the fermentation process.

Malted and unmalted barley

In this sauna-like climate, the barley grains were turned constantly, which is why the workers wore platform shoes – similar to the ones that are in fashion now and during the 1980's. These shoes were necessary to prevent burns to the feet, but hey, why not look stylish while being safe? An especially important moment in the barley turning process was to time it exactly, so that each batch was of the highest quality.

Visually, you would hardly see a difference between the malted barley and the untreated one, however, if you were to try it, you would notice that the treated grain tastes sweet and poppy.

The germination process comes to a natural halt with the help of hot air. Nowadays, most distilleries purchase the finished product from commis-

sioned companies that specialise in malting. This takes away from the tradition in my opinion, but perhaps, makes the end product more abundant.

Working in the barley houses was a popular trade and provided some additional health and beauty benefits. In those days not everyone owned their own bath, so they took opportunity where they saw it and bathed in the barley! I know, I know, there's the whole question of hygiene, but they were different times back then, with different worries. As we are now living in a time where there are significantly more baths to be found in Ireland, you don't need to worry that malt houses will become the local swimming hole on a hot summer's day!

THE MILLING AND THE MASHING

At this point the differences in whiskey production between Ireland and the rest of the world will become more apparent.

Clockwise: Water mill wheel, Kilbeggan Distillery, Kilbeggan - Mill stone, Kilbeggan Distillery, Kilbeggan - Mill stone, Tullamore D.E.W. Old Bonded Warehouse, Tullamore - Old Barley mill, Slane Distillery, Slanecastle Demesne

As mentioned before, a special tax for malt barley was introduced in 1661. Because of this, the Irish started to mix untreated barley with sprouted barley. This mixture is malted together and all parts, including the skin, are passed over to the next step where the real fun begins.

During the mashing process, there are two important things to observe: the timing has to be exact and the temperature of the water which the barley is soaked in, needs to be just right. Every distillery has their own way of doing things, but the goal of this process is to wash the starch out of the barley. After the bath, the fluid and the remaining mass are separated from each other. The liquid – called 'wort', is sent to the fermentation and the remaining mass – the mash, was in the past left for the farmers who fed it to their cows. As I have learned, some distilleries still practice this, just like in the old days. Perhaps this could be one of the reasons for the unique taste of Irish butter and while this is not a book about Irish butter, I recommend a taste.

THE FERMENTATION

The aim of the fermentation is to convert the starch from sugar into alcohol. The liquid from the step before – the wort – is essentially nothing more than beer without hops, just like a knock-off beer. Liquid yeast is added to it and pumped into a fermentation tank – the so called 'washback'. Every distillery has its own secret recipe for the fermenting. The yeast at this point will ferment the sugar to alcohol and carbon dioxide. As the amount of yeast

Mash tun, Walsh Whiskey Distillery, Royal Oak, Carlow

results in different tastes, the fermentation process is meticulously observed so as to achieve a certain standard.

In the past this was done by tasting, smelling and a visual inspection, whereas today, a computer tracks the optimal course of the fermentation. During this process the temperature will reach between 260 and 320 degrees Celsius (500 and 608 degrees Fahrenheit). The fermentation process lasts between two and three days and the result is an alcohol content of 10%.

There are still distilleries out there which rely on the senses of their employees instead of the assistance of a computer, so if this seems like the job for you I say 'Go for it! Follow your heart!'

THE DISTILLATION

The fermentation process produces an alcohol called 'weak beer'. During this step, it's put into the pot still and the temperature is brought up to 78⁰ C. The upper part of the pot contains wires which lead the developed vapours into the spirit receiver where they will be converted back into liquid form.

During the first round, the alcohol solution, the so called low wines, contains about 20% alcohol. In this step, the alcohol as well as most of the odorous substances and flavouring are separated from the water. The liquid at this point is still observed by an employee just to make sure all boxes are ticked.

Pot stills, Royal Oak Distillery, Royal Oak, Carlow, Co Carlow

During this process, the alcohol is separated into three parts for the distillation: the first and third parts go back and are mixed with the newest fermentation liquid, while the second part is used in the next process. For this step, there is a special tool which looks like a glass box with a switch.

The distillation master watches, smells and tastes the outcome of part three, known as 'the heart' and transfers it to the second copper pot, the 'spirit still'. Again, a distillation process takes place in this pot, which results in a 70% alcohol level. Here you can see another difference to the Scottish whiskey production – Scottish Whiskey is usually only distilled twice.

Some Irish distilleries also end the distillation process here, however, traditionally a third distillation process takes place in a third copper pot.

With the third round, an alcohol level of 85% is reached. This is the very alcohol the whiskey will be made out of.

My driver Shem and I were taking part in an event called 'Whiskey Live' which takes place every November in Dublin and as part of that exhibition where we enrolled into a master class at the Royal Oak Distillery. We were given the opportunity to taste the pure pot still made from malted and non-malted barley containing 80% alcohol. Up to this point I had always assumed that the smooth taste originated from the barrel. I was more than surprised to find out that alcohol distilled in copper pot stills already held this characteristic taste, which develops through the triple distillation and the chemical process formed

Spirit safe, Tullamore D.E.W. Old Bonded Warehouse, Tullamore, Co. Offaly

between alcohol, heat and copper. Some distilleries sell this drink under the name poitín. For those of you who cannot wait three years to taste real Irish Whiskey, this would be a fast solution and a tasty one.

During the 18th century the tax was calculated from the amount of whiskey that was gained after the last distillation process. As a result, the tax men were placed in the distilleries as permanent fixtures. I spoke with one of these tax men who worked during the 1970s in the Jameson distillery. He reported that even at this time the production was monitored 24/7 to avoid tax fraud. Nowadays the production amount is overseen by a computer. The last distillation is run through a counting mechanism where the correct tax rate is automatically calculated.

Phrase definition
PURE POT STILL

Irish whiskey (Pure Pot Still, Irish Pot Still) consists of a mixture of malted and unmalted barley which is triple distilled in a copper still. This method is unique and is solely used in Ireland. This way the whiskey receives a much more complex aroma leaving this wonderful creamy taste for the drinker to enjoy. The choice of barrel for the ripening process will refine the taste, colour and smell of the whiskey.

THE COLUMN STILL

In 1830, the demand for Irish whiskey was so high, that the manufacturers were in search of a method that could shorten the production time. The idea of Scotsman Robert Stein was to distil the liquid in a tower-like construction instead of copper pots. This idea was finally improved and brought to the market by Irish man Aeneas Coffey. This method is known under different names, like Coffey Stills (after Aeneas Coffey) and Column Stills (because of the tube like still). At the end of the day it doesn't matter what it's called, the principle is the same: instead of numerous stills, only one long vertical tube is used in which the alcohol can be distilled continuously and without interruption.

The main advantage of this method is that clearly less effort is needed. Several steps are no longer required - like the cleaning of the stills and the transferring of the solution into the next pot. The column still works constantly and without the same level of intervention, thus production around the clock is possible. Additionally, the steel which is used for the tubes is much less sensitive to corrosion than the copper that is used for the pot stills, as copper and alcohol react. The last, but nonetheless important point, is that other grains like rye, wheat and corn can be used.

The invention of Stein and Coffey was thoroughly thought through, and even today, 200 years later, the world cannot do without the column still method. It is used universally and not only in whiskey production, but also for the manufacturing of vodka and other spirits. However, this quicker and cheaper method does – thankfully some might say – neither create the aroma, nor the flavourful depth that is reached by using the pot still method. This is mostly due to the fact that by using such a quick way of processing, many flavours don't even reach the distillate. Furthermore, after finishing the first distillation step, the pot still method uses only the core part – the best piece – for the next part, whereas the inferior, less tasteful parts remain in the distillate of the column still procedure.

THE MATURATION

The gained alcohol can be used as a base for all sorts of drinks, like vodka, London gin or poitín. For gin you would just need to add berries (often juniper) or herbs, as it is done, for example, in the Glendalough Distillery. At this

Jameson Distillery Bow St. Museum, Dublin

point in the whiskey distillation process the produced alcohol is too strong to drink, so it is thinned down with water to approximately 63% and poured into barrels. From this point on it's a game of patience and also punctuality, because you're going to be waiting for three years and one day until you can drink a real Irish whiskey. Although whiskey is the star of the show, there needs to be some recognition given to the barrels!

After all it is these barrels that partially give whiskey its colour; that exotic, but rich taste; and its reminder of the past when wooden barrels were still used for storing whiskey. Each distillery utilises different barrels in different ways. Depending on how the whiskey is stored i.e. vertically, on palettes or even on sand like in the Echlinville Distillery in Northern Ireland, due to the effect of temperature variations (there is a reason for everything). Even nowadays it is common in Ireland to utilise used barrels for the maturation process. For the production of bourbon (whiskey in the USA) it is required by US law to use only new barrels made from white oak. Normally bourbon is only stored for one year in this barrel, after that it is not allowed be used again. In the 16th century, the export of used whiskey barrels from the USA to Ireland and Scotland began for this very reason.

The liquid acquires part of the taste and colour of the barrels. Before the barrels are filled, they are repaired, cleaned and 'burnt out' from the

inside. This burning is responsible for the caramel flavour, and the vanilla taste originates from the US oak wood barrels. Barrels that were used previously to store port, sherry or madeira for an average duration of three years are also put to use, which help contribute to a very distinct aroma.

During the maturation process, the whiskey loses 2% of its volume each year, sad to say, but it's a good thing. At first it was assumed that the staff were secretly tasting the whiskey, but later it was discovered that a portion of the alcohol evaporated. The Irish are historically both poetic and religious, obvious through the naming of this evaporated alcohol as 'Angels Share' - a wee portion for the angels!

As Irish whiskey is required to mature three years and a day, 6% of the alcohol will already have evaporated by the end of this term. The older the whiskey gets, the better the taste – and the more expensive

Cask staves, Tullamore D.E.W.

it will be. If you think about all the effort that goes into the production, the price is a little more bearable.

In the past, as well as nowadays, there are different ways to sell whiskey on the market. The best solution for a distillery is to store it in its own warehouse. Another option is that a private individual, a pub or a trader purchases the whiskey and either stores it in the distillery or in their own storehouse. In order to level the playing field, small and bigger distilleries alike will engage in either using private or public resellers. During the course of whiskey history, there have been quite a few distilleries who didn't produce under their own brand name, but instead produced for others, making the mystery around whiskey all the more real.

Dingle Whiskey Distillery, Co. Kerry

WHISKEY BONDING – THE REINVENTION OF THE FORMER ART OF WHISKEY MATURATION

At the peak time of the whiskey production in Ireland there were many distilleries, but not many variations in the taste of what was being made. As we know by now, whiskey is not cheap and it is a trade that involves patience. In order to make money you have to spend money, or so the saying goes. It was not uncommon in the past to sell a part of the freshly produced whiskey, sometimes even all of it to tradespeople, or in Ireland, a so called 'bonder'. This helped distillers maintain cash flow while selling a less developed product in order to invest in the time-consuming whiskey. In most cases the merchants that bought this 'fresh whiskey' had several shops/ businesses, for example Corrigan's Pub in Castleblayney, Co. Monaghan. This businessman owned a grocery shop, a funeral home, a hardware shop, a cobbler shop, a wood, steel and coal trade and last, but not least, he also held a license to sell alcohol. The whiskey bonder took the barrels away for storage, was responsible for the refining part and finally, filling the bottles that he would later go on to sell. The same whiskey, probably made on the same day would be transferred to the different counties of Ireland and go into storage there.

As external circumstances play an important role in the storing of whiskey, the initially identical produce could vary greatly after 4 years of maturation with different bonders. Depending on, for example how salty the air was, or if there were apple trees near the storehouse, then the aroma and taste of the whiskey would be influenced. As a delightful consequence, many varieties of different whiskeys were created. Actually, every Irish place or town claimed that its whiskey had its own unique taste. Unfortunately with the downfall of the distilleries, this particular feature of Irish whiskey production died out as well.

Now, 100 years later, there are efforts being made to revive the 'bonder tours', only this time it's not the liquor dealer wanting to expand his selection, but whiskey enthusiasts who want to do their part and help to bring the 'golden drink' back to its former glory.

You can still spot bonder signs at old buildings or pubs, for example:

The Old Coch Inn, Castleblayney, Co.Monaghan
Corrigan's Pub, Castleblaney, Co. Monaghan

Currently one of the most popular bonders in the Irish market is

Different maturation stages of whiskey

Chapel Gate Whiskey, which is bringing the old tradition back to Ireland. As recently as 2016, the first whiskey barrel was 'bedded' for maturing at the family farm in Co. Clare. The idea behind it was to bring old, forgotten brands back to life. Chapel Gate recently brought their first whiskey 'The Gael' to the market and have already been rewarded with golden awards.

↗ chapelgatewhiskey.com

THE MARRING AND VATTING

These days several distilleries are beginning to go back to their roots and make 'Pure Pot Still Whiskey' to add to their brand. Another trend cropping up is blended whiskeys, which are the results of the mixing of different distillation methods. The blending is the last step in whiskey production.

Working cooperage, Kilbeggan N91 CY54, Co. Westmeath John Neilly,

In the 18th century, Irish whiskey producers were still fighting fiercely against the blending of different distillation methods and they took legal action against it, however, they were defeated.

Today though, it's seen as an art requiring a lot of skill to blend the whiskey in such a way that it is a pleasure to smell the aroma and a delight to taste the end product.

THE MEANING OF SINGLE POT STILL, SINGLE MALT, SINGLE GRAIN AND BLENDED - *A small overview of the technical terms*

People with either no or little knowledge about whiskey can often feel overwhelmed by all the different terms and phrases. To prevent any confusion, I will explain some of the most important definitions. In general, the following is crucial for whiskey: the manufacturing type; the distillation method; the age and the type of barrel used to store it.

SINGLE MALT

This type of whiskey is made in a distillery and is produced from one type of grain. In Ireland and Scotland this grain is malted barley. Single Malt does not tell you anything about the distillation method, the age of the whiskey or the barrel type it's been stored in. There are many different outcomes for whiskeys branded as single malt, for example:

Triple distilled: *Bushmills 10-years-old-Single Malt,*
Tullamore Dew 14-years old
Single Malt or twice distilled: *Glendalough 7-years old,*
Teeling Single Malt, Connemara 12-years old (with peat aroma)

POT STILL/ PURE POT STILL/ IRISH POT STILL

These whiskey brands are exclusively produced in Ireland and consist only of malt and a mixture of malted and non-malted barley. They are triple distilled in copper pots. Today traditionally produced whiskeys are still available.

I would recommend trying *Green Spot, Middleton, Powers, Redbrest* or *Paddy Centenary.*

GRAIN WHISKEY

Grain whiskey is produced by using rye, wheat and corn. As corn cannot be distilled on its own, a small proportion of barley or another grain needs to be added to react with yeast. Since barley crops do not fare as well in the United States as they would in Europe, the Americans predominantly use rye, wheat and corn as a base for their whiskey. The most popular Irish grain whiskeys are *Kilbeggan 8-Years-old Single Grain* or *Teeling Single Grain Red Wine Cask Finish.*

BLENDED WHISKEY

Here we are dealing with a mixture of different types of whiskey (pot still, column still or single malt), however, it's also possible to mix whiskeys of the same type that hold a different age or that were matured in different barrel types, which will create a new sort of whiskey. The aim here is to reach a certain colour, a specific taste or a consistent aroma. The original idea was to increase the volume of an expensive product with cheap alcohol. Today, blending is certainly an art form. Another reason the image of blended whiskey is so distinct is that each whiskey producer wants to create a unique beverage, therefore nowadays, blending has very little to do with watering the whiskey down. Jameson is one of the leading Irish distilleries producing blended whiskey – their newest creation is called *Jameson Cooper's Croze*.

CASK FINISH

This is one of many methods to create a whiskey with a specific aroma. At the end of its maturation, often for the last 6-12 months, the whiskey is stored in a barrel that previously contained, for example, madeira or sherry.

CASK STRENGTH

The alcohol content in a bottle of whiskey is usually between 40-43%, which is seen as 'drink strength'. Cask strength whiskeys have the alcohol level from when the whiskey was in its barrel, for example Writers' Tears Cask Strength is at 53%.

FINALLY, THE MOST IMPORTANT QUESTION – HOW TO PROPERLY TASTE A WHISKEY?

There are many so called 'gurus' out there who want to educate the unknowing on how to properly taste a whiskey. Along with Shem (my local driver), I came to the conclusion that you just have to try and see what tastes good to you and at the end of the day, the whole process is very individual. It goes without saying that it is important that you like whiskey.

During our journey we gave every whiskey a chance and a taste.

Here are some personal tips for beginners which will tell you what to be aware of if you are on a taste discovery tour and want to be able to clearly judge. It's always good to drink some water to neutralise the palate, thereby cleansing your taste buds from previously enjoyed food or drinks and to get it ready for new impressions.

Whiskey testing in the Dublin Bar Academy in Dublin

For the experts there are 4 criteria to test the whiskey: the colour, the aroma, the taste and the palate.

First, the colour is examined, which could vary from bright yellow to deep red with as many variations in colour as you can get in pieces of amber.

The next step is the smell or finding the aroma. The best whiskey glasses or so called 'nosing glasses' are tulip shaped, so you are able to swish the liquid around. The glass can be brought up very closely to your nose, so you can absorb the aroma as much as possible. Often advertisements suggest that whiskey should be enjoyed with ice, however, this is only recommended for American whiskeys which were produced with the column still method and were only matured for one year. You can also add ice to Scottish whiskeys with their smoky flavour. For Irish whiskey you don't need ice. Quite the opposite. With pure barley whiskey, for the best result, warmth should be added to the whiskey. This will be achieved immediately by swirling the whiskey in the glass, which allows the warm air to infiltrate the whiskey. You will notice instantly how the aroma ascends. It is similar to cognac tasting, where glasses with big, round middle parts and a small exit hole are used. The alcohol rises much more quickly than the air to the top. If you additionally warm the glass with your hands, you will be rewarded with a wider variety of aromas. Now you are ready for the best part – take a sip and taste the whiskey. As a rule of thumb, you should hold the whiskey in your mouth a second for each of its maturation years before you swallow it. This way the smooth, round and sweet flavour of exotic fruits will unfold more and more, and the aroma palette increases.

Whiskey Testing in Dylan Whisky Bar, Kilkenny

At last, the outflow or aftertaste is assessed. The outflow is what happens after you swallow the whiskey. The whiskey leaves a warm taste either in your mouth, in your throat and/or in your belly. With every sip you will discover a new aroma and your taste buds will exult in different ways. With even a drop of water added with a pipette, a new taste or aroma will develop.

I have found various descriptions of the same product's taste from different online suppliers, which goes to show that at the end of the day, taste is quite subjective. That doesn't mean that you have to smell and taste all of these flavours and aromas. Most people can only experience a fraction of what the experts taste and interpret into a whiskey.

*May the luck of the Irish lead to happiest heights
and the highway you travel be lined with green lights.*
Irish toast

Before we start our journey

A BIT OF GENERAL INFORMATION ABOUT IRELAND

The history of Ireland is traceable 6,000 years, right back to the Megalithic culture. Over this extended period many towns, villages and small communities were founded and strongly influenced at different times by the Celts, the Vikings and the British. These folks didn't always come with peaceful intentions and often colonised the people. It took the British 800 years until they finally said farewell to the Island and even then, they kept six counties (still a sore subject for some). Irish history has a long and emotional, often sad and marked background.

Let's start with a few basic facts. The total area of the island measures approximately 84,421 km² which is comparable to the size of Austria or Bavaria (70,550 km²). About 70,283 km² belongs to the Republic of Ireland, the rest is Northern Ireland which forms part of the United Kingdom. At the longest point Ireland is 486 km long and 285 km at the widest point. You will

Irish road sign. Name on the top is in Irish and below in English. The blue sign with white waves is the special marking for the Wild Atlantic Way

36

find the Irish Sea to the east and this divides Ireland from Britain. In the west, you find the Atlantic – keep on going and the next stop is America.

Many people are curious as to why I decided to live in Ireland. Some key factors for me were that it is an English-speaking country and it's surrounded by the sea which is perfect for sailing. The last fact is especially important if you want to be able to explore and discover new shores at any time. But the sea is only a part of Ireland's fascinating landscape. The face of Ireland is shaped by beautiful mountains, hills and valleys that rival the beauty of any other land.

A typically Irish narrow road

It doesn't matter whether you are in Dublin, Cork or Galway, you'll rarely be far from the sea, where you can relax at one of Ireland's 365 beaches. If you want to go hiking in the mountains, paddling on the river or just enjoy the peace and quiet – everything is close by or a few minutes outside of town, however, I have to admit that Ireland is not really suitable for skiing and snow lovers. I have heard of people who dared go skiing in the mountains in Co. Wicklow, but don't forget the winter here rarely lasts more than about 10 minutes.

In 2017, the police (Gardaí) were forced to put up roadblocks between Co. Wexford and Co. Carlow because it had been snowing that morning and too many families with small children came to see the snow and build snowmen! The permanent west wind brings fresh air from the Atlantic (there will never be a shortage of this ocean breeze). You are simply in the right place for sailing and all other kinds of sport where wind is necessary. Ireland is famous for two reasons: it's very green and it is always raining. Colm Tóibín (author of the book 'Brooklyn') describes in his book 'Surviving Ireland' seven different kinds of rain. His categorisation is the following: 'Soft Days, Spitting, Regular Rain, Lashing, Bucketing Down, Limerick Rain and Sideways Rain'.

I want to go into a bit more detail about two of them: 'Soft days' are days where fog and mist last the whole day. 'Sideways Rain' means the rain is coming from the side. For this type of rain you won't need an umbrella, as it comes with a strong wind, which will make it impossible to hold your

Wicklow Habour, Wicklow, Co. Wicklow

umbrella in place. The best case scenario is that you will get wet anyway, the worst case scenario is that you hurt yourself while fighting with the umbrella. For any type of rain in Ireland make sure to buy rainproof clothes.

Because of the high amount of rain and the moderate climate – with an average of 5–10° Celsius (41–50 Fahrenheit) in the winter and 15–20° Celsius (59 to 68 Fahrenheit) in the summer, Ireland is known as the 'Emerald Island' or 'the green Island' and legend has it that the Irish can describe '50 different shades of green'. The famous American singer, Johnny Cash, missed a few and wrote the song, 'Forty Shades of Green'

No matter where in Ireland you tour, or where you stop during your trip, you'll almost always be able to enjoy a postcard view. So many times during our travels while researching whiskey, we simply had to stop at the side of the road to admire the beautiful views, thus delaying the next taste for just a little while.

For such a small country, Ireland is a great place to lose your way. The many narrow roads and winding ways that lead you through valleys and over rivers are entrancing in their beauty, but don't let this lead you astray. Although the island looks small from above, Ireland is anything but. There are plenty of winding roads and valleys for you to discover and enjoy. To save you some trouble from potentially getting lost without the help of GPS, I've gathered some helpful tips.

In my home country Germany, we like to name the same place multiple times and then add the name of a nearby river to differentiate it. Ireland like Germany uses the same naming practice, but without the handy nearby river name to distinguish it, for example 'Frankfurt am

Main' or 'Frankfurt/Oder' (both Main and Oder being rivers). This sounds confusing and yes, it is at first, but there is some sense in the nonsense. Here cities and towns are attached to the county they are in, which more times than not is easily noticeable by the locals' accent or county colours on flags and buildings. The county, often shortened to 'Co.' is simply added to the name of the town. For example, there is Aughrim in County Wicklow (on the east coast), but there is also a second Aughrim in County Galway (west coast), where in 1691 an important battle took place.

Post codes were only introduced to Ireland in 2014, yet have still not really taken off. To make it a little more challenging, addresses often include only the name of the town/city and region. I often had to drive to appointments where the company didn't have a 'proper' address that I could enter in to my GPS. The Irish, having grown up with this system barely notice it, whereas me being the detail-oriented German that I am, need to know everything exactly as it is. Although the island is small, some places are obviously bigger than others – take for example Co. Meath and Co. Cork – go look at a map and you will see what I mean. Some town names exist in three different counties. This can drive you a little bit mad, especially if you are sitting in your car and you just want to type in the address into your GPS and get there.

Glendalough Monastic Site

To make all this even more exciting, the Island is divided into two - Northern Ireland and the Republic of Ireland and four Provinces: Ulster, Leinster, Munster and Connacht. To shine some light into this chaos, we will start with the provinces.

THE IRISH PROVINCES

Ireland is divided into four provinces. This division originates from former times, when the island was divided into different kingdoms. The provinces are called Connacht, Leinster, Munster and Ulster. In former times there was also a fifth province, Meath, which is now a part of Leinster. If you have a look at a map you will see that Meath is not very big, however, in the past Meath was the home of Kings and the capital of the island, which has probably something to do with its geographical position, close to the hill of Tara – I will explain more about this later. Today the provinces are especially important for rugby, hurling and Gaelic football fans. In all other areas, like administration and civil service for example, that became less important over time. One reason for this could be that after the loss of the six northern counties and the formation of the Republic of Ireland, the respective governments took over these tasks.

Every province is divided into counties. In total there are thirty-two counties, twenty-six of these are located in the Republic of Ireland (and are therefore under Irish rule), and six of them belong to Northern Ireland (therefore under British rule). It's a handy political thing to know, especially for visa regulations and also so you don't unintentionally offend anyone by claiming they are the same thing.

Since 1922, the Province of Ulster is home to two regional parts, Northern Ireland and the western part of the Republic of Ireland. The title 'Republic' was given to the 26 counties only in 1949 – before this it was referred to as the 'free state'.

Map by 'Clocha na hÉireann' or 'Stones of Ireland' - monument erected in Glencolmcille in Donegal

ULSTER is located in the north of the Irish island and is generally known to be rugged and full of dramatic landscapes. Northern Ireland consists of the counties Antrim, Armagh, Fermanagh, Down, Derry and Tyrone with the counties Cavan, Donegal and Monaghan belonging to the Republic of Ireland.

Carrick, Co. Donegal

The remaining provinces are located in the Republic as follows:

CONNACHT is positioned in the western part of Ireland and is part of the beautiful coastal route known as the Wild Atlantic Way. This province is especially popular with tourists and many of its inhabitants still use the Irish language in areas called the 'Gaeltacht'. Connacht consists of the counties Galway, Leitrim, Mayo, Roscommon and Sligo.

Ben Bulben, part of the Dartry Mountains in Co. Sligo

LEINSTER is situated on the east part of the island. This province has the highest population of all the provinces, because Ireland's capital and biggest city Dublin is located there. In the past this part of Ireland was well sought after and had an abundance of jobs, meaning many people left the countryside to settle here. In Leinster you find counties Carlow, Dublin, Kildare, Kilkenny, Laois, Longford, Louth, Meath, Offaly, Westmeath, Wexford and Wicklow.

Sugar Loaf Mountain, Co. Wicklow

MUNSTER is home to many of Ireland's artists and musicians. Whether it's the ever-changing scenery, the light or the weather, many painters and writers gravitate to West Cork and Kerry. Similarly, Clare seems to hold a great attraction for those who play traditional music. Munster stretches across the west coast of Ireland over the middle and into the south. The counties belonging to Munster are Clare, Cork, Kerry, Limerick, Tipperary and Waterford.

Typical coastline, Co. Clare

And just so you the beloved visitor stay on your toes, there is the added complication that a place and a county can have the same name. For example, there is County Donegal as well as the town Donegal, County Kilkenny and Kilkenny as a city. In addresses this is partly highlighted, for example: Cork, Co. Cork, or Wicklow, Co. Wicklow. When in doubt always clarify whether a person means Wicklow the town or Wicklow the county.

Most tour guides follow the geographical division of the counties. If you are driving from Dublin to Galway (from the east to the west), you will most likely cross six different counties. That is why I have added the name of the counties to each address in this book. Additionally, I have included the GPS coordinates to make this journey as simple and enjoyable as possible for you, or maybe this is the highly-detail oriented German in me coming out? Who knows!?

Misty outlook to Wicklow Gap

ARRIVAL OPTIONS AND GETTING AROUND

There are three different kinds of transport options to bring you to Ireland: the plane, the train or the ferry.

BY PLANE: The main airports are located in Dublin, Cork and Shannon in the Republic of Ireland and Belfast for Northern Ireland. For domestic flights there are additionally the airports of Galway, Kerry, Sligo and Waterford. Most tourists travel to Ireland via Dublin airport.

EUROSTAR – VIA BRITAIN WITH THE TRAIN: For those who dislike planes, the Eurostar is a good alternative way to reach Ireland, especially if you want to stop in England and Wales on the way. In the summertime it's advisable to book your train tickets well in advance.

VIA THE IRISH SEA: If you would like to take your car, bike or camper van with you to Ireland, the ferry is the best option for you. Ferries depart from both Great Britain as well as France and Spain. You can find ferry terminals in Belfast, Cork, Dublin Port, Dun Laoghaire in south County Dublin, Larne Co. Antrim and Rosslare Co. Wexford.

These are the main connections:

from *Fishguard (Wales)* or *Pembroke (Wales)* to *Rosslare*
from *Holyhead (Wales)* to *Dublin Port* or *Dun Laoghaire*
from *Liverpool (England)* to *Dublin Port*
from *Swansea (Wales)* to *Cork*
from *Cairnryan (Scotland)* or *Fleetwood (England)* to *Larne*
from *Stranraer (Scotland)* to *Belfast*
from *Cork* to *Santander (northern Spain)*
from *Roscoff (France)* to *Cork or Rosslare*
from *Cherbourg (France)* to *Rosslare*

Please check the ferry timetables before you make plans to travel to ensure they are running to schedule, as weather can affect the routes/timetables Additionally, be mindful of the journey length when you plan your trip. Please find the web sites of some popular ferry companies:

↗ faferry.de, ↗ poferries.com, ↗ irishferries.com,
↗ fastnetline.com, ↗ norfolkline.ferries.org, ↗ stenaline.ie

CURRENCY In the Republic of Ireland the currency is the Euro and in Northern Ireland it is the British Pound Sterling.

DIRECTIONS Ireland only recently introduced the use of postcodes. Usually an address only consists of the name of the town and the county. For navigation systems, it is not always easy to locate places in Ireland. If you are asking somebody for directions, get ready to be told a whole story about the place. The directions you will be given could refer to churches, pubs, schools and hospitals. I personally give up after the first pub, as I cannot remember all the information anyway. My advice is to get good roaming internet from your local telephone provider or a prepay sim-card, so you have access to online maps.

PUBLIC TRANSPORT The public transport in Ireland is not as bad as some would say, however, I would not compare Irish cities to Berlin, Barcelona or London. The public transport options in Ireland are more or less Dublin orientated, that means if you look at the map, all routes lead to Dublin. Tickets for the train and for Bus Eireann (the provincial bus service) can be purchased on the appropriate websites, or from apps in the app store. You can purchase bus tickets directly on the bus, but you will need to have exact change, as you will not get your change back, so always bring lots of small coins. Additionally, you can pay for all public transport with a 'Leap card' (electronic prepaid card). If you plan to stay longer in Ireland and use public transport often, this will be an ideal alternative to the constant search for small change. The Leap card costs €5 and is available in all small shops and newsagents, where you can also top the card up if need be.

THE TRAIN There are two main railway stations in Dublin City: Connolly and Heuston. Trains operate from Dublin to Belfast (north east), Galway (west), Rosslare (south east) and Cork (south). Connolly station is the place of departure for all trains north and for the east coast. From Heuston Railway Station trains run in the directions of Galway and Cork. The trains are comparable to other European rail standards.

Iarnród Éireann/Irish Rail

Tickets can be bought both on the official website ↗ **irishrail.ie** and at the railway station. Please note that some routes are only served four times a day, for example from the east coast to the southern part, therefore, I'd advise checking the timetable. The coastal city train in Dublin is commonly known as the 'DART' – Dublin Area Rapid Transport – and operates between north east Dublin to north County Wicklow. The route between Dublin centre and Greystones runs along the coast and offers a beautiful view over Dublin Bay. Going the other direction, from Dublin centre heading north, it will bring you to the sailing and fishing town of Howth. Please be aware that the DART operates only once an hour on Sundays and Bank holidays.

LUAS Luas (Irish for 'speed') is the tram system in Dublin. There are two different lines: Green and Red. Both of the tram lines meet in the city centre and on O'Connell Street, near the General Post Office (GPO). Though they don't intersect, there is a short connecting tram line. The stops are about two minutes apart. Many stops out-

Luas, a tram/light rail system in Dublin.

46

side of the city centre have a park and ride facility (P+R), which greatly helps those city commuters avoid the city traffic jams and reduces overall congestion. Tickets are available at machines at the stops or you can use the Leap card as previously mentioned. There are different ticket options like single ticket, day card, family card or multiple days tickets. For more information, visit the website at: ↗ **luas.ie**

Bus If you don't have a car, the bus is one of the easiest ways of getting around. Buses travel regularly, even to the most remote areas of Ire-

land. The only difficulty you might encounter is finding the bus stop, due to the fact that they are often not properly marked. To be on the safe side, use bus stops that you can find on maps. Important to know is that the bus won't stop just because you are standing at the bus stop, so you'll also have to indicate by

Bus Éireann/National Bus

sticking your hand out that you would like to get on. Tickets are available on the bus, on the website or at the bus station before departure. The website of the state-owned provider is ↗ **buseireann.ie.**

The main bus station is Busaras in Dublin city centre and while many intercity busses depart from here, the privately-operated ones usually leave from the Dublin Quays. There are also some bus companies that are often a little cheaper and offer you more options to get around in Ireland:

JJ Kavanagh & Sons ↗ **jjkavanagh.ie** (to Dublin airport from Kilkenny, Waterford, Clonmel, Portloaise, Nenagh, Carlow and Limerick).

Matthews ↗ **matthews.ie** (you'll find ideas for day trips here)

City Link ↗ **citylink.ie** (City Link connects cities like Galway, Limerick and Cork).

AIRCOACH These transfer busses operate 24 hours, 7 days a week. This bus company is not only useful in getting to and from the airport, but also to travel between cities. Information and timetables can be found on ↗ **aircoach.ie** On the webpage ↗ **dublinairport.com/to-from-the-airport/by-bus** you will find other bus companies that are recommended by Dublin airport, however, I haven't tried all of them yet.

DUBLIN BUS The buses in Dublin operate regularly, but only stop if you indicate by holding out your hand that you want to get on. Tickets can be purchased on the bus, therefore you need to bring small change. Please be aware that bus drivers won't accept notes and will not be able to give back any change. More information about this can be found under ↗ **dublinbus.ie.**

CAR If you are planning to discover Ireland with a rental car, please don't forget your EU driver's license or have an international permit that allows you to drive abroad. You should clarify with the car rental company if you are allowed to drive in Northern Ireland, or, if you start your journey in Belfast, you are allowed to travel around the Republic of Ireland in the rented car. Please note that people in Ireland, like in the UK, drive on the left side of the road. The driver's seat will be on the right

Looking for a pub in the Wicklow Gap

hand side of the car. It took me a while to get used to having the gear stick on the left hand side. I would often look for it on the right and hit the car door with my hand. If you want to save yourself from that hassle, just get an automatic car.

The motorway system is pretty clear. All bigger cities are connected by motorways. Not on all routes, however, will you find a petrol station. The situation has improved in the last five years, but nonetheless I would advise you to always have enough fuel in your car. The same goes for scenic regions like Donegal, Mayo or the Wicklow Mountains – you can drive for many kilometers without passing a house, not to mention a petrol station.

It is important to know that you have to pay a fee to use some sections of the motorway (it is called 'toll'). There are toll stations on exiting where you can pay the road charge directly, however, there are 2 exceptions: the M50 which is the Dublin ring road (charge point is on the northern part of the M50 between exit Lucan and Blanchardstown) and also if you use the Dublin tunnel.

These parts of the motorway are facilitated with electronic toll devices and can be paid by calling (1890 50 10 50) – though most filling stations and convenience stores can accept payment. You can also pay at their website (ì eflow.ie). Be aware that you have 24 hours to pay the e-tolls, so don't forget or your rental company could slap on a fine!

These are the 8 most important toll stations: M50 (barrier free with electronic toll collection), M1 (Gormanston – Monasterboice), M3 (Clonee – Kells), M4 (Kilcock – Enfield – Kinnegad), N6 (Galway – Ballinasloe), M7/ M8 (Portlaoise – Castletown/Portlaoise – Cullahill), N8 (Rathcormac – Fermoy Bypass) and N25 (Waterford City Bypass).

Wicklow Head

Useful Information on Irish Life, Hospitality and Food

Ireland and the Irish The Irish are a friendly folk, very relaxed and welcoming – the terms 'easy going' and 'laid back' describe this pretty well. This is probably why they are not so good at accepting criticism. Conflict as we all know is stressful and uncomfortable, but I think here we have a special case with the Irish. A simple example was an occasion when I left most of my meal on the plate in a restaurant. Rather than ask me if everything was ok, the waiter simply avoided eye contact when removing my plate and turned his attention instead to Shem with his very empty plate and asked him if everything had been satisfactory. A small thing, but grrrrr!!! very irritating, yet if looked at in another way, it does have a certain cultural charm.

I think it's quite rare to hear an Irish person say 'no' or complain much, which is also a positive thing. I have included some tips in this book, which may help you to avoid potential awkward surprises. I am sure that you'll be better able to navigate certain situations knowing that it's just a case of possible cultural misunderstanding. Hopefully you will see the funny side of it. I do find that the Irish compensate for their lack of service culture with their friendliness and kindness.

LANGUAGE There two official languages: English and Gaeilge. I've been told I should call the latter 'Irish' as only foreigners refer to it as Gaeilge. Irish and English are two languages that have different ranking here in Ireland. English is used as the common everyday language, while Irish is taught as a subject in schools and spoken commonly only by small pockets of the population. In some regions, for example in parts of Galway, or 'Gaillimh' in Irish, you can experience the language first hand. These regions of Irish speaking places are known as 'Gaeltacht' areas. It is

Signs are in both English and Irish

mandatory to learn Irish in school and all civil service jobs, e.g. police, teachers, government administrators must have a certain level of Irish. Throughout the Republic of Ireland the road signs and place names are written in both languages. In the last few years, there has been an increased interest in Irish abroad and in Ireland itself, with Irish speaking schools (called Gaelscoileanna) and Irish names for newborns springing up more and more.

THE IRISH WEATHER There is nothing more exciting than the Irish weather. As a friend of mine once said – 'If you don't like the weather, just wait ten minutes until it changes again'. The weather in Ireland changes rapidly, that's why the Irish dress themselves according to the 'onion principle' – layer after layer of clothing. They might wear a thin jacket, a thicker jacket over that and maybe an even bigger jacket over this one too. The most important thing, however, is a windproof rain jacket. This one must be neither too thick, nor too warm. Not too thick as you might need to take it off again after 10 minutes and put it into your bag. By the way, you can forget about using an umbrella. Due to constant wind which will regularly change direction, you would probably spend

more time trying to rescue your umbrella from the wind than protecting yourself from the rain.

ACCOMMODATION The cost of accommodation in Ireland will very much depend on whether you decide to go for a city break or stay in the country, for example, accommodation in Co. Clare can be as little as €25 per person including breakfast. In the rest of the country you are looking at prices from about €70 per double room per night. For cities like Dublin, Cork, Galway or Belfast, a reservation is definitely recommended.

Accommodation like hotels, hostels and bed and breakfasts (B&B's) are often in high demand in these cities, both in the summer and in the winter. Accommodation in the surrounding areas of Dublin and Galway is often fully booked too. Outside of the bigger cities you will find many small hotels and beautiful B&B's. I personally enjoy the B&B's in the countryside where you'll get a real Irish welcome, something that I always

feel whenever I stay at one. Here you will experience the Irish hospitality first hand and with a little chit-chat from the owners, you can find out all the local information about what to see in the area, where to eat and whatever else you have in mind.

It's probably a good idea when checking in to ask how the shower

The Glenmalure Lodge, Glenmalure, Co. Wicklow

works. Some have a heater switch which might be located outside the bathroom and others, a cord from the ceiling. You don't want to find yourself standing in the cubical with cold – or no water coming from the shower head.

You will also most likely need an adaptor to charge any device you may have, as the sockets are different to European and American ones (they are the same as those used in Great Britain. Ireland uses 220v, so don't fry your hairdryer if it works off 110v!

The following websites can help with accommodation searches

➚ ebookers.ie ➚ airbnb.com ➚ hrs.de ➚ privatestay.com,
➚ donegalcottageholidays.com ➚ irishlandmark.com,
➚ manorhousehotels.com ➚ irishcountryhotels.com

FOOD It is worth pointing out that a lot of dishes on offer contain beef or lamb, just a heads up. The animals graze for between eight and nine months of the year or, in some areas, the whole year round. This results in an excellent quality of dairy and meat, however,

Lunchtime, sandwich and a pint

the vegetable offering tends to be very limited. If you are ordering a traditional meal you will usually find some cooked vegetables, like potatoes, carrots, cabbage, turnips and parsnips. I won't say it's impossible, but its rarer to find a fresh salad accompanying a dish like a roast.

Vegetables and fresh salads are often not up to the standard of those in warmer countries. The Irish climate is not suitable for many kinds of vegetables and salads, as they don't get enough warmth from the sun. Nowadays, of course everything can be imported, but in the traditional Irish kitchen these 'exotic' vegetables don't play a major role. Just be aware that what can be called salad, can often be anything mixed with lots of mayonnaise, like coleslaw.

Another small thing that I often find, is a meal is rarely served the complimentary bread you might be accustomed to abroad. Unfortunately, it only seems to appear when soup is ordered. This might sound odd, but

Irish Breakfast

there have been times when I've ordered an appetiser like pâté or goat's cheese and it was served without bread. Be safe friends and ask for bread if you'd like some.

While I'm speaking here in general terms, there is a big move to improve the situation and more imaginative food can be quite easily found – you just need to look a little harder. Trip Advisor would be useful here: ↗ **yelp.ie**

If you stay in a B&B, you will most likely be treated to a traditional Irish breakfast to start off your day. This is also referred to as a 'Full Irish' and in Northern Ireland it's called an 'Ulster Fry'. There a many regional differences in breakfasts, but because of the large variety I'll leave that for you to find out. Traditionally you are served fried rashers, pork sausages, fried eggs (or scrambled egg), white pudding and black pudding, fried tomatoes and toasted sliced bread or traditional Irish soda bread. Sometimes they offer you sautéed mushrooms, as well as baked beans in tomato sauce or hash potatoes (hash browns). This dish is often served throughout the day in many pubs, restaurants and coffee shops. It is a very rich and satisfying dish – almost too much so – you may not need to eat again until the following day.

Some B&B's in popular tourist regions now offer alternative breakfast dishes, but to make sure you're not disappointed, just ask the evening before what is on offer and if you have special dietary requirements, suggest an alternative option. In most cases the owner of the B&B will be happy to accommodate you. Lactose-free and gluten-free food is also available in every big supermarket in Ireland.

Flannerys Bar in Limerick

THE PUB One of the most important social institutions in Ireland is the pub. In former times the pub didn't just serve drinks, but was also a shop, whiskey trader, funeral home and much more under the same roof. Primarily though, it served the people as a second living room. This function remains even today. One can meet up with friends for a 'pint', mostly beer, and 'Craic' - pronounced 'crack' (which is Irish and means 'fun' and has nothing to do with drugs). There is live music in most pubs and visiting musicians will often spontaneously join in.

It's far from uncommon in Ireland to get your instrument out of your bag and play some tunes. Everybody gets his or her chance to show off their skills. And once the music is playing, it won't take long for the people to sing along and dance. Don't be shy in a pub! The Irish love to talk, so it won't take long before they involve you in a conversation. This will happen even faster if you are sitting at the bar.

Tea Tea for the Irish, as with whiskey, serves as an all-encompassing medicine for all kinds of situations. It doesn't matter what has happened or is going to happen, the first thing an Irish family will do is to make a good 'cuppa' tea. Irish tea is quite strong, as it is normally diluted with a little to a lot of milk, depending who is drinking it. Don't be surprised to get two or three tea bags if you order a teapot. General rule of thumb: the cosier the pub, the bigger the teapot.

Before we start our whiskey journey through Ireland, a few last words. I have included some newer distilleries that did not have visitor

Tea and scones – a traditional afternoon favourite

centres at the time of writing. Many distilleries buy alcohol and store it in order to modify the taste of the whiskey. Others produce spirits like vodka, gin or poitín and store a certain amount of their production. Even if these distilleries currently don't offer whiskey, you can see in what direction the produce of each individual distillery may go in the future and you can look forward to the first whiskey that these distilleries will bring to the market. I personally think that the small, owner led distilleries are much more interesting than the larger and well-known ones. That is why I would like to encourage you to give the lesser known whiskey brands a try and really 'get to know them'.

> *'That the sound of happy music, And the lilt of Irish laughter,*
> *fill your heart with gladness, that stays forever after.'*
> Irish toast

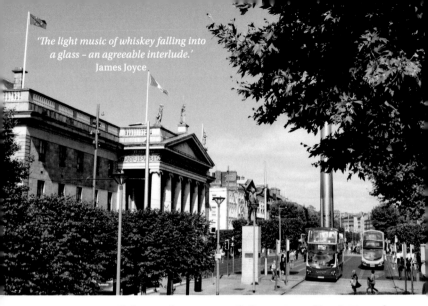

'The light music of whiskey falling into a glass – an agreeable interlude.'
James Joyce

Dublin – 'Town of the Hurdled Fort'

Dublin is the biggest city and also the capital of the Republic of Ireland. The Irish name is: Baile Átha Cliath [ˈbalʲɑːˈkʲlʲiə] or [ˈbʲlʲɑːˈkʲlʲiə], which translates to 'Town of the Hurdled Fort'. The English name comes from the Irish word Duibhlinn [ˈdivʲlʲiːnʲ], 'black pond '.

Dublin city has a population of about 500,000 which is really not that big. The Irish always mention numbers around 1.2 million as Dublin's population, but that's including county Dublin which is like including all the different little towns that make up London or New York.

Before we dive into the history of Dublin whiskey, I first want to give you some alternatives that involve more than just driving around and enjoying a glass here and there. Dublin is a big city teeming with non-stop traffic, just like all other big cities and here we have the problem that you, the reader, will be driving on the, what might be to you, wrong side of the road. This though should not be a problem as driving a car in Dublin City is something you'd only do if you

Dublin by bicycle

really have to. Even Shem, my 'no excuses' driver thinks there are better ways to explore the city. One of these is to rent a city bike, which should be no problem, because they have pick-up points throughout the city.

↗ **dublinbikes.ie**

As good as this option is in theory, just be aware that Dublin city generally does not cater to cycle lanes and that whiskey tasting and cycling maybe isn't the best combination. If this option isn't for you, no worries, Dublin has public transport, like Dublin Bus and the Luas – an excellent tram service.

With the Luas alone, you can reach the following distilleries: Pearse Distillery, the Jameson Museum and the Irish Whiskey Museum. All the other locations for this part of the tour can either be reached by bus or on foot. This will also give you different perspectives on how you see the city. The best option in my opinion is the 'Hop on and Hop off' Bus tour.

Shem and I personally tried both the Red and Green routes and found that whiskey places of interest could be reached using this type of travel. Both routes are offered to tourists, but my personal opinion was that the Red one was not especially well structured.

The Green route does a better job in my opinion. There isn't much difference in the prices of either. Both offer 1 and 2 day ticket options and most of the typical tourist spots are covered with both. This is probably one of the most cost efficient and quickest ways to see a lot if you're on a budget or tight for time.

The 'Hop on and Hop off' bus is my recommendation. In the book I focus on the spots that have significance to Irish whiskey.

Hop on Hop Off Bus

↗ **dodublin.ie**
↗ **citysightseeingdublin.ie/hop-on-hop-off/**

General Post Office, Dublin

The tours start on O'Connell Street not far from the GPO (the General Post Office). This is a historical building that played an important role in the 1916 uprising. On the first part the tour, you'll be brought to the docklands, where you'll see the new Dublin port area. With a lot of modern architecture mixed in with some Irish historical buildings and other points of interest, places like the Customs House, the Jeanie Johnson Famine Ship and EPIC, the emigration museum. My favourite is the Samuel Beckett Bridge. It was built in the shape of a harp. The harp is also one of the national symbols of Ireland. The bridge stands beside some of the more architecturally interesting parts of Dublin. As you drive through the streets, you'll pass many of the preserved Georgian houses, the colourfully painted front doors which you'll no doubt see on postcards.

The numbers on the bus stops are not chronological, so I recommend keeping the map you get with the ticket. At bus stop 3 is Trinity College Library. Here you will find the famous 'Book of Kells', a work that was produced by monks around 800 AD. If you do go and see it, you'll surely wonder at the extraordinary skills they had in those darker days.

↗ **tcd.ie/library**

Irish Whiskey Museum, Dublin

Only a few steps away, you can find a most interesting museum, the **IRISH WHISKEY MUSEUM**. The Museum is located centrally in Dublin city opposite the main entrance of Trinity College. The Irish Whiskey Museum is independent of the drinks industry and so they are able to offer an impartial point of view. Their mission is to celebrate the story of Irish whiskey, reclaim Ireland as the original home of whiskey and to ensure that that part of Irish History will not be forgotten.

During the tour, you will get a good historical overview of all things whiskey, as well as fun little anecdotes about Dublin. The tour also provides a good insight into the Irish way of life and how the Whiskey Industry influenced many aspects of it. Of course, you'll also get an opportunity to try whiskeys from different distilleries around the country as part of the various tours on offer.

For the admission price of our tour, you got to try three to four different sorts of whiskey. For only €3 extra, you can upgrade to their Premium Tour, where you will receive a free whiskey glass and an extra whiskey to test. Not a bad way to start a whiskey tour around Ireland, or a great way to finish it!

What I particularly enjoyed was the Candlelit Tales storytelling. We sat back and relaxed over a drink or two as our guide regaled us with stories of Irish mythology and legend. Throughout my years living here, I have noticed that the Irish do storytelling well, so what a great way to enjoy classic Irish lore, traditional Irish music, and whiskey! Heaven.

Irish Whiskey Museum, Dublin

If you need a quiet place to relax after the hustle and bustle of the busy city, the contemporary bar upstairs offers tea/coffee, some mighty fine Irish whiskeys, Irish Coffee and a good selection of whiskey cocktails, all while taking in the beautiful view of the grounds of Trinity College below. On Fridays, Saturdays, and Sundays they offer an interesting and unique "Whiskey and Brunch Experience". The brunch offers a tour of the museum followed by whiskey tasting and Irish smoked salmon with bread and delicious Irish Whiskey marmalade!

📍 *Irish Whiskey Museum, 119 Grafton Street, Dublin 2, D02 E620, +353 1 525 0970,* ↗ **irishwhiskeymuseum.ie**

Around the corner you'll find Bus Stop Number 4. From there, you are just five minutes away from the stop that will take you to the heart of the Irish whiskey world, located in the Liberties (Irish: 'Na Saoirsí', sometimes also called 'Na Libirtí') just like it was back in the 1800s. The translation means 'free' or 'freedom', depending on the context. This part of the city was on the outskirts of the city walls and therefore the residents of this area didn't pay tax, hence the meaning of 'free'. The full name of this area was Liberties St. Patricks Cathedral and it primarily housed Dublin's poverty stricken population. The Liberties was well known for its street markets and small family businesses which were, in the 17th century, also famous for producing wool and silk products. In the 18th and 19th Centuries, this area developed into a whiskey haven for those wanting to try their luck at distilling. Formerly at the edge of the city, the Liberties has now been absorbed in to the city and is really not far from the centre of Dublin.

'.iberties
build-
, CATHE-
PATRICK'S
12). There
,niskey distiller-
., that the place was
. the 'Golden Whiskey
. This corner was founded
.he three resident distilleries
of Roe, Powers and Jameson. The
reason for deciding on this part of
the city was not coincidental. For
the production of whiskey, having a source of freshwater is of the
utmost importance, however, the
water from the River Liffey is partially a mix of sea water so that
would not do. Thankfully there was
another option to be found in the
waters of the River Poddle. This river comes from the Dublin hills and
was used as a water reserve for the
south part of the county. That's how

Christ Church Cathedral, Dublin

the Liberties became this golden area of whiskey production. At the high
point of the whiskey boom, there were never less than forty distilleries
here at a time.

The four most important distilleries in the golden corner were:
John Jameson & Son on Bow Street, William Jameson & Co. on Marrow-
bone Lane, John Power & Son on John's Lane and George Roe & Co. on
Thomas Street. These distilleries all produced high quality whiskey using all the new technologies that the turn of the century created. The
focus for these distilleries were on purity, quality and tradition. This
meant sticking to the practice of distilling in the single pot fashion and
not changing to the new column still method. As it happens, this would
be one of the reasons that only two out of the four distilleries survived
the changing times.

Jameson has kept its visitors' centre on Bow Street since it opened.
Today you can still find two active distilleries – Teeling and Pearse Irish

Whiskey, which like Jameson's, you can also visit. As of 2018, two additional distilleries – the Dublin Whiskey Company, an one across from the Guinness Storehouse (stop 13) and on the of the George Roe Distillery. Thus, the old tradition begins to modern times and Dublin, once again, finds itself at the peak of production.

Directly at bus stop 12A, you can find the **TEELING DISTILLERY**, located in the Liberties. The motto of the distillery reads 'Back to Roots', basically back to the glorious times of the past.

Teeling Distillery

The building is constructed in a new and modern fashion, but with many references to the past. The Teeling brothers, although having founded the distillery only recently, have a long and detailed background in whiskey. In 1782, Walter Teeling founded Dublin's Marrowbane Lane Distillery which was then later bought by their neighbour, William Jameson & Co and then later, managed by family members of John Jameson. In 1923, the business closed. The father of Jack and Stephen would later go on to found the Cooley Distillery and lead it on to the success it enjoys today. His sons continue to advance the knowledge of the Irish whiskey traditions into the 21st century. In this distillery the whiskey is produced in the older fashion and is distilled three times. There are also three beautiful copper stills to admire. A sweet gesture is that the three stills are named after the family's daughters: Natalie, Rebecca and Alice.

Like at most other distilleries in Ireland, the curious drink of poitín is also produced here, alongside other small batch whiskey variants. Because I am a person that likes just about all whiskeys and not just the ones stored in bourbon barrels, I am all for the Teeling Single Malt. The distillery rounds off its excellent selection of whiskey by also offering wine sorts like Sherry, Port, Madeira, Pinot Blanc and even a Cabernet Sauvignon.

The tour will take you through the stages of its whiskey production. This way you can see all the small and intricate details that go into the

The Bang Bang Barby Teeling Distillery, Dublin

making of the various products. A visit to Teeling whiskey will be most informative and memorable.

📍 *Teeling Whiskey Co. Visitor Centre, 13-17 Newmarket, Dublin 8*
D08 KD9, +353 1 531 0888, ↗ teelingdistillery.com

In 2019, just around the corner from the Teeling Distillery, the **DUBLIN LIBERTIES DISTILLERIES** will soon begin production and the distillery will be opened at the same time as their visitor centre. The Brew Master Darryl McNally, brings with him over twenty years of experience in the whiskey business. The whiskey that will be produced here will use peat, which will give it a different taste from the others. This should provide cocktails with an interesting twist on the old. Now I'm going to let you in on a small secret: the visitor centre will also have a 'Bar Experience' which will gladden the heart of every cocktail lover. This alone makes me very excited to see what will come next from this newcomer!

♥ *The Dublin Liberties Distillery, Visitor Centre, 33 Mill Street, Dublin 8, D08 V221*

↗ **dublinlibertieswhiskey.com**

The Dublin Liberties Distillery

JAMESON BOW STREET DISTILLERY is located beside the number 20 bus stop. It was founded in 1780 and therefore, belongs to one of the oldest whiskey distilleries in Ireland. In 1886, this distillery was located on about five hectares of land. In those days the distillery was located on Bow Street where the visitor centre is now found. In 1971, the four resident distillers of the Irish Distillers Group (Jameson, Paddy, Power, and Midleton) decided to move production work entirely to Midleton, Co.Cork from where they still operate today.

The Bow Street Distillery, Dublin

In its heyday, the Bow Street Distillery was a sizeable place, almost like a small city within the city. In addition to the distillery, there were many craftsmen nearby, including blacksmiths, carpenters and painters. A key reason that many businesses found themselves in this part of town is once again due to the close proximity of freshwater. Originally, the area was surrounded by oak forests which gave the whiskey produced here a rich and oaky taste.

Bar in The Bow Street Distillery, Dublin

John Jameson ranked quality as one its highest priorities. The whiskey giant had stringent controls and processes for how and from where it sourced the barley used in production. The prices might have been a little higher than most, but his customers were those that valued the quality and came back for more. John Jameson had cellars in which the temperature and the moisture of the room would be kept just right during the ripening process. In the golden age of whiskey in Ireland, these cellars would house around 25,000 barrels, which made the yearly production of whiskey around 1 million gallons, making this distillery the second largest in Ireland. A former tradition at the distillery was that visitors could fill up their own bottles with whiskey. This 'Cask Strength Whiskey' could not be bought anywhere else in the world and the bottle was registered with a name so that it could be tracked.

📍 *Jameson Bow Street Distillery, Bow St., Smithfield Village, Dublin 7 D07 V57C, +353 1 807 2355* ↗ jamesonwhiskey.com

Staying in the area and just around the corner is the former church of St. James Street, which shut its doors in 1954 and was later bought by the company Alltech. In this old building, across from the Guinness Brewery, the **PEARSE LYONS DISTILLERY** has decided to make their mark. The church was built in 1268 and later, in 1539, when King Henry VIII closed all the catholic churches and cloisters, this church was rededicated as a

Pearse Lyons Distillery in the old church, Dublin

protestant one. Dublin's main cemetery was also located here during the 18th and 19th centuries. Unfortunately, in 1948 a fire destroyed the church's original tower. It's no coincidence that the president of the company Alltech, Dr. Pearse Lyons, founded his distillery here. His grandfather John Hubert Lyons, along with eight other family members were buried in this cemetery. It would be easy to assume that this particular piece of land held a special place in his heart. The distillery currently operates with two copper stills that you can be sure look as beautiful as the rest of the building.

Pearse Lyons Distillery in the old church, Dublin

📍 *Pearse Lyons Distillery/Alltech, St. James's Church Distillery Visitor Centre, 121-124 James's Street, Dublin 8, D08 ET27, +35316916000,* ↗ **pearselyonsdistillery.com**

The **JOHN'S LANE DISTILLERY,** also under the name of John Power & Sons existed from 1791 till 1974. In his description, our friend Alfred Bernard said that it was one of the nicest and most effective whiskey distilleries in Dublin. In his book he dedicated six pages to it, docu-

menting his excitement and overall praise for the Dublin business. Founded in 1791, the distillery produced a mere 6,000 gallons of alcohol per year. Some forty years later, the figure rose to 300,000 gallons a year, even overtaking their competitor Jameson in 1871. With fresh water being one of the most important ingredients for whiskey, they chose to source theirs from the Vartry River. Powers Whiskey distilled the typical Irish whiskey: distilled three times in the pot still fashion and with a mix of malted and unmalted barley. The area surrounding the Jameson Bow Street Distillery was filled with small businesses and artisan workers. One special thing to note is that the distillery was conveniently located next to a fire station, a good thing given the propensity for fires to break out near such businesses.

In 1866, the Powers Distillery was the first in Dublin to start bottling their whiskey. By doing so, a customer could be sure that their whiskey was pure and not mixed with other elements by those who might otherwise tamper with its quality. The bottle represented a gold standard amongst distillers and with this they could cement their brand even further, which was the case with Powers Gold Label.

Unfortunately, after the move was completed in 1974, not much remained of the old distillery. Today, in the former grounds of the distillery you will find the National College of Art & Design. In the garden of the school, you can still take a look at one of the remaining copper kettles.

John's Lane Distillery from 1791 till 1974, Dublin

About a thirty-minute walk from the school you can find the old Jameson Distillery. Powers Gold Label is still one of the most popular drinks in pubs around Ireland today. It's a bit sad to say that Powers Gold Label was, in the past, thought of as the 'poor man's whiskey', but in my opinion the taste is flavourful and bold. Powers Gold Label is now produced by the Irish Distilling Group in Midleton, who continue to distil it in the old way – pure pot still. For me, this brand is every bit as good as its brother, Jameson.

♥ John's Lane Distillery (National Collage of Art and Design),
Thomas Street, Dublin 8, D08 K521, +353 1 636 4291

The part of the wind mill from Roe & Co Distillery, 1757 to 1923, Dublin

The **ROE & CO DISTILLERY**, located opposite the Guinness visitor centre, will open a new distillery soon. It will be remembered for being one of the biggest and most famous breweries of the 18th century. The George Roe Distillery was located from 1757 to 1923 on Thomas Street. When our friend the writer Alfred Bernard visited in 1866, the production rate of the place was around 2 million gallons a year. This was double the amount of what Jameson produce today and would go on to make it one of the biggest whiskey producers worldwide. This distillery was so successful that the sons of George Roe donated £250,000 (£2.5 million pounds in today's money) for the rebuilding of Christ Church Cathedral after it was destroyed by fire. Despite their success, however, the giant whiskey label began to feel the effects of change and the influence of cheap whiskey blended in Scotland which saw their sales drop.

The force of such events eventually led to the lawsuit together with Jameson, DWD and Bushmills to argue the case of pure pot still whiskey. Unfortunately, this lawsuit was lost and due to the consequences of economic changes, whiskey production ground to a halt there in 1923. Today this distillery is remembered through the adverts you can still find in pubs around the island and by looking out at the old windmill across from the Guinness factory. This windmill was built in 1757 and is one of the oldest of its kind in Europe. Its height lends it one of the best vantage points for visitors to see most of Dublin's skyline.

The opening of the Roe & Co Distillery is a joyous event for the Diageo Group and can

Whiskey from the new Roe & Co Distillery

perhaps bring a piece of Ireland's whiskey history back to life. One regret in my opinion, is that the whiskey here will be a mix of grain and malt whiskey, which ironically was one of the main reasons this distillery didn't survive in the first place.

The whiskey itself will be stored in old bourbon barrels and will have an alcohol content of 45%. As for taste, I think it will be a great compliment to many cocktails due to it not having the traditional strong taste of an unmixed whiskey. This will be the first attempt of the Diageo Group to produce a whiskey of their own. I'm excited to see what comes from this distillery and am hoping for an imminent announcement of the secret location of the visitor centre.

Celtic Whiskey Shop, Dublin

And lastly, a few tips. Directly beside the number 7 bus stop, you can find the **CELTIC WHISKEY SHOP**. It's located right in the middle of Dublin and is a specialty shop for wines and whiskeys. Here you can find every whiskey that is produced in Ireland and there is no question you can ask that the staff won't be able to answer. The Celtic Whiskey Shop is also the organiser of the event 'Whiskey Live', which takes place every autumn. An excellent place to find all of Ireland's whiskey producers and their products under one roof.

📍 *Celtic Whiskey Shop & Wines, Green 27-28 Dawson Street, Dublin 2 D02 E066, +353 1 675 9744,* ↗ celticwhiskeyshop.com

MITCHELL & SON WINE MERCHANTS is a spirit's business that has been run by the same family since 1869. The initial reason for the business was so that the Mitchell family could buy up whiskey to bottle it later and sell it under their own name. You can find the traditional product under the name of 'Green Spot' and the business is still flourishing today.

📍 *CHQ Building, IFSC, Docklands, North Dock, Dublin 1, D01 R9Y0 +353 1 230 2301,* ↗ mitchellandson.com

The **PALACE BAR** is located in the Temple Bar area and is one of the oldest pubs in Dublin. The establishment retains its old Victorian style, giving the visitor an idea of how it looked in a bygone era. Just like in the past, you can still find a wide assortment of quality Irish whiskeys there.

📍 *Palace Bar, 21 Fleet Str, Dublin 2 D02 H950, +353 1 671 7388*
↗ **thepalacebardublin.com**

Palace Bar, Dublin

Another interesting bar is **THE OAK**. It's located in the middle of old historical buildings, but has been renovated in a modern Georgian style, all the while still offering a classy whiskey selection. Here you can also find old Powers whiskey advertisements.

📍 *The Oak, 1-4 Parliament Street, Dublin 2, D02 AN28, +353 1 671 8267*

The Dingle Whiskey Bar

The **DINGLE WHISKEY BAR** takes its name from the popular peninsula in County Kerry. At the time of writing, there weren't many whiskeys you couldn't find there. It's an interesting and beautiful place and close to Trinity College in the city centre.

📍 *The Dingle Whiskey Bar, 44 Nassau St., Dublin D02 YY44, +353 1 677 4180*
↗ **theporterhouse.ie**

The **JAMES FOX CIGAR AND WHISKEY STORE** used to be a tobacco shop. Now you can purchase both whiskey and cigars. You can also find a good selection of smaller 50ml bottles – handy for the traveler. Here you can try the whiskey before buying it, which to me is a sign of good customer service.

📍 *James Fox Cigar and Whiskey Store, 119 Grafton St., Dublin 2, D02 E620, +353 1 677 0533,* ↗ **jamesfox.ie**

Ryan's of Parkgate Street, Dublin

RYAN'S OF PARKGATE STREET is an original Victorian public house located near the front gate of the Phoenix Park. Made famous for pouring one of the best pints in Dublin, it's now also gaining a reputation for its popular oyster bar. At Ryan's you can still see many of its original Victorian features such as gas lamps, whiskey barrels, tea drawers and traditional snugs. The barmen are slightly more recent.

📍 RYAN'S F.X.BUCKLEY, 28 Parkgate Street, Dublin 8, ↗ fxbuckley.ie

THE BRAZEN HEAD is one of the oldest pubs in Ireland and was a meeting place for historic rebels. This brass-filled, lantern-lit pub hosts live music every night.

📍 The Brazen Head, 20 Lower Bridge St.
Merchants Quay, Dublin 8
D08 WC64, +353 1 677 9549
↗ brazenhead.com

The Brazen Head, Dublin

If you have some extra time before or after your whiskey tours and want to experience the beautiful Irish countryside, I would recommend an organized day trip. I found "Irish Day Tours" to be very good. Trips like the Cliffs of Moher, Wild Connemara, the Giants' Causeway, Blarney Castle & Cork, Kilkenny & Wicklow, and many others are on offer.

You can sit back and listen to your guide while being driven around the stunning Irish countryside.

Day Trip with Irish Day Tours

71

And now a little something special to end on 'Imported to Dublin and Dublin whiskey history'. **REDBREAST** is a very good example of the life of a whiskey bonder, both historically and right up to the present day. It's among my favourites and could become one of yours. It's one of the most famous whiskeys to come from the house of Irish Distillers in Mildelton and its story is an interesting one.

Advertising for Redbreast Whiskey

Wine merchants or 'bonders' **W&A GILBEY** came from London to Dublin in 1861. They had their warehouses on Dublin's Harcourt Street. Today the company is based in O'Connell Street. Like many bonders at the time, they bought whiskey from a distillery and matured it in their own sherry casks and sold it to consumers under their own labels.

In 1870, they had 300,000 gallons of whiskey in stock. The name Redbreast was first given to the whiskey in 1912. Before that, it was sold as 'John Jameson & Sons Castle, JJ Liqueur Whiskey 12-Year-Old' in a bottle which had pretty much the same shape as today's Redbreast's bottle. Gilbey's chairman at the time was an avid birdwatcher and gave it the nickname after the little Robin Redbreast so popular on Christmas cards. Like the bird, the name was met with fondness and in 1912, it officially became Redbreast.

In 1985, Gilbey's ceased production of Redbreast and in 1986, it entered into an agreement to sell the brand to Irish Distillers. It was an immediate success when relaunched in 1991, after several years of absence from the market.

I honestly believe that this might just be the best single pot still whiskey there is. It has the smoothest taste and a true sherry flavour. Today you can buy four different versions of the Redbreast limited edition. Definitely one of my favourites is the Redbreast

Redbrest testing at Whiskey Live in Dublin

12 Year Old Single Pot Still Irish Whiskey which will bring you to whiskey heaven. You HAVE to try it!

↗ redbreastwhiskey.com

THE JONES' ROAD DISTILLERY (1873–1945) was one of the six biggest distilleries in Dublin. One of the interesting things about this distiller, was that it did not have its origins in a family business, but was instead the creation of seven different businessmen. It is said that during the height of its production, it produced 560,000 gallons of whiskey a year. The quality and purity of their products was a very important consideration for the distillers and in the Jones' Road Distillery, they only practiced the pure pot still method. Unfortunately, like many distillers in the country, they had to close their doors, though you can still find their advertisements in pubs across Ireland. In place of the old building, there are now apartments.

DWD Whiskey

I was delighted to hear that in 2014, the Dublin Whiskey Company acquired the rights to the old name. Just as it did in the past, the business has begun to buy whiskey bondings and sell them under their own name. Unfortunately, it is not yet known if a distillery will be created under the traditional name, but the 'Heritage D.W.D.' can already be purchased from specialist retailers.

↗ dwdwhiskey.com

*"Too much of anything is bad,
but too much good whiskey is barely enough."*
Mark Twain

Short trips into the outskirts of Dublin

In case you don't want to venture too far out of Dublin, or if you don't have enough time for longer trips, I have gathered some interesting sight-seeing possibilities in the following chapter.

The North of Dublin

For the area to the north of Dublin I have picked out two different tours for you. The 'Slane Tour' is more of a day trip and especially fascinating for travelers who are interested in history, architecture and geology. The second tour brings you to the Cooley Peninsula and offers many scenic landscapes, as well as even more whiskey and is therefore also suited as a weekend trip.

The Slane Tour

Slane Castle and Slane Castle Whiskey Ltd. are enjoyable tour destinations. Located in the Boyne Valley, County Meath, close to the Hill of Tara, Slane Castle is still a family owned property which was constructed in 1785 by James Gandon, James Wyatt and Francis Johnston. It was restored in 2001 and has been accessible to visitors ever since. Here, those with an appreciation of castles can admire the popular Gothic Ballroom designed by Thomas Hopper, enjoy the architecture and the garden or relax in the castle's café. Occasionally, large events with international stars take place. Acts like the Rolling Stones, Bob Dylan and Bruce Springsteen have all performed here.

Slane Castle, Slanecastle Demesne, Slane, Co. Meath

In September 2017, the whiskey distillery also opened its doors to visitors. We had a chance to look at a few areas and get a first impression of what the distillery has to offer. It is located in the coach house, where the horse-drawn carriages in days gone by were housed and where the horses were cared for and where today the famous golden liquid is made. The distillery is an exciting mixture of old and new, as many of the old rooms were kept close to their original design and converted to a new purpose. For example, there is now a bar in the former stables. Where previously horses slept and ate, you can now enjoy cocktails in a stylish atmosphere. With Shem, I selflessly tested some of them for you. What I found most interesting is how well they managed to integrate the old buildings with the new distillery in such a harmonious way.

Slane Distillery, Slanecastle Demesne, Slane, Co. Meath

At the time of writing, the distillery was not yet three years and one day old, so the whiskey on offer had been bought in and matured in barrels. Here though, they do achieve their own unique flavour as they use three different barrels. For their brand 'Slane Castle Whiskey', the liquid is refined by letting it mature, firstly in a 'virgin oak' barrel – (an unused oak barrel), then in a barrel that has been used to store Tennessee Whiskey, and finally in a

former Oloroso Sherry barrel. The whiskey will adopt a variety of exotic aromas as well as a hint of caramel and vanilla through this process. I look forward to a taste of the whiskey that they are now distilling themselves and perhaps, by the time you visit, it will be ready. Through the castle, the distillery and the village of Slane, you will get a fair impression of how Ireland might have looked in the past.

Slane Castle Whiskey Distillery

📍 *Slane Castle Whiskey Distillery*
Slane, C15 XP83, Co. Meath,
+353 41 982 0643, ↗ slanecastle.ie

Travel on for about another 20 km from Slane and you will reach the 'Hill of Tara'. The Hill of Tara, off the M3, is a hill in County Meath, on which you can find numerous prehistoric and ancient monuments. The hill is known from the time of the legendary King Cormac Mac Airt, who ruled in the 3rd century AD, however, it is assumed that this place was, for a long time before that, of religious and Celtic importance. Legend has it that the High Kings of Ireland had their seat here. As a guarantor for the social and cultural unity of the provinces of Ireland, Tara was and still is one of the most important symbols for Irish national unity and identification.

In the old classic Southern States' movie 'Gone with the wind', Tara had an important role in so far as the O'Hara family plantation was named after this mystical place in Ireland. The main character, Scarlett O'Hara, grew up in Tara and returned back to her Irish birth place at the end of the movie. In the sequel 'Scarlett' in 1994, Scarlett O'Hara travels back to Ireland. As she visits the 'real' Tara, Scarlett picks up a handful of soil to bring back to America in order to scatter it over the grave of her late father, a native Irishman.

📍 *OPW, Hill of Tara Visitor Centre, Dunsany, C15 P44W, Co. Meath*
+353 46902 5903, ↗ heritageireland.ie

Hill of Tara, Dunsany, Co. Meath

If you are in this area, you should definitely see the UNESCO World heritage site 'Brú na Bóinne' (Newgrange), which is located only 25 km – about a 30 minute drive from Slane and the Hill of Tara. 'Brú na Bóinne', which means 'Palace of Boyne' in Irish, or more specifically 'palace of the white cow', is situated in the Boyne Valley, north of Dublin in County Meath. Here you can find a large amount of prehistoric Celtic sites, which originate from around 5,000 years ago. Several of them are very well preserved. Among these is a large grave mound hill surrounded by megalithic stones. In 1933, it was inscribed as a UNESCO World heritage site.

♀ *Bru na Boinne visitor centre Newgrange and Knowth, Donore, A92 EH5C, Co. Meath, +353 41988 0300, ↗* worldheritageireland.ie

From this point onwards, you can either go back to Dublin or, if you have more time, travel further north to visit the Cooley Peninsula.

Hill of Tara, Dunsany, Co. Meath

THE COOLEY PENINSULA TOUR

The distance between Dublin city centre and the end of the Cooley Peninsula is about 120 km. If you intend to visit all of the following places, you should definitely plan at least two days for this. Even if you are only in Ireland for a short trip, this tour will give you a wonderful insight into the diversity of the Irish landscape.

The Cooley Peninsula has a lot to offer and legend has it that it was the scene of an ancient power struggle resulting in the story 'The Cattle Raid of Cooley', in which the best bull ever born was stolen. The story involves Queen Medb and Cú Chulainn and is possibly the best 'bull' ever told.

From here, you will have a spectacular and varied landscape. The peninsula stretches from Carlingford Lough in the northwest to Dundalk Bay in the south over an area of approximately 60 square miles. This is a scene of mountain chains, flat fertile plains, wide valleys, dense woodland and long beaches. The former inhabitants of the peninsula left their traces everywhere, so there are lots of clues as to how they used to live.

The following tour includes several distilleries on the Cooley Peninsula. The first place I'd recommend to stop is the town of Drogheda, which is situated about 50km north of Dublin in Co. Louth. Drogehda is one of the oldest cities in Ireland and is filled with majestic buildings dating back hundreds of years. Moreover, you will find here a beautiful cathedral and a fascinating museum. This town has a lot to offer those who are interested in culture. There are also plenty of atmospheric pubs and restaurants, however, we are more interested in two places, the Boann Harvest Distilling and Brewing and the Listoke Distillery & Gin School, Listoke.

The **Boann Distillery** is situated in the heart of the Boyne Valley and is the property of the Cooney family. This distillery has the philosophy that any raw ingredient has to be natural and also from the local area. Thus, the water for the whiskey is sourced from the Boyne Valley and the wheat is grown locally. Naturally the care invested into choosing the basic ingredients, which are of the highest quality, transfers into the taste of the end product. While the distillery values traditional processes on the one hand, it uses all

Boann Distillery, Drogheda, Co. Meath

modern possibilities of recycling on the other. For example, the heat produced is used to run the packaging lines as well as heating the restaurant, the visitor centre and the office. Rainwater is also collected and utilised. The visitor centre is still under construction, therefore it would be advisable to check on their website whether it's open to visitors.

The distillery currently offers several types of whiskey: Single Malt, 10-Year-Old-Single Malt, 7-Year-Old Blue Note, and 7-Year-Old Cask Strength.

📍 *Boann Distilling, Lagavooren Platin Road, Drogheda, A92 X593 Co. Meath, +353 41 987 8078*
↗ boanndistillery.ie

The **Distillery at Listoke** is found close to Monasterboice, the ruins of an early Christian monastic settlement. This distillery uses the most up to date techniques and equipment. Visitors have the possibility to create their own gin in a workshop. Whilst that's not whiskey, the production steps are very similar, and you are allowed to keep the bottle with your homemade gin.

📍 *Listoke Distillery & Gin School, Unit 9, Tenure, Tenure Business Park, Co. Louth, A92 XP70, +353 87245283*
↗ listokedistillery.ie

If you still haven't had enough whiskey and gin by now, you can travel further to Dundalk which is 40 km away. Dundalk and whiskey have a common past and it looks as if they will also share a common future. The old building of the **MALCOLM BROWN'S DISTILLERY** (1800–1925) can still be viewed from the outside. There is also an old granary and in the former malt house you will now find a country museum, the tourist office and a public library. The museum offers a general overview of the region's history, but unfortunately you will not find much information about the distillery.

Malcolm Brown's Distillery

In my search for more information, the museum staff advised me to a go to a very interesting pub, the **WINDSOR BAR AND RESTAURANT**. The building I found through this insider tip was built in 1893 and was the seat of the **MCARDLE MOORE BREWERY**. Today it is home to a Victorian style pub and restaurant. If you have some time left, you should definitely go and visit these beautiful rooms. By all accounts you will find a huge variety of whiskey – and if you are lucky, you might get the opportunity to chat with the owner who took over the property from his father and knows a lot about the history of the town.

Windsor Bar and Restaurant, Dundalk, Co. Louth

♀ *Windsor Bar and Restaurant, Dublin St. Townparks, Dundalk, Co. Louth,*
+353 429338146

The **GREAT NORTHERN DISTILLERY LTD** was a beer brewery in the past, but has been transformed into a whiskey distillery in the last few years. Founded in the late 16th century, it only moved to its current location in 1896. You can still admire the original architecture of the old office buildings. The distillery produces alcohol for different clients and sells both pure alcohol and longer stored whiskey. Customers who intend to bring their own brand whiskey to the market, can purchase the whiskey here, refine it themselves and bottle it as their own brand. Dr. John Teeling (more info to come) founded his second Independent Distillery here. The first one he built in the 1980s on the Cooley Peninsula, only a few kilometers from Dundalk.

He brought it to success and sold it to Jim Beam in 2013. As you can see, this pioneer of the new Irish whiskey era didn't let the grass grow under his feet, he just repeated his success. In this distillery, anybody, no matter whether you are a business man or simply want it for your personal consumption, can purchase a barrel of whiskey, store it there and fill it into your own bottles. If you don't want to buy a whole barrel, you can start with a bottle of their very limited line, Burke's.

Like many other distilleries which are located outside of Dublin, the Great Northern Distillery is situated at the bottom of the idyllic Cooley Mountains as you can see for yourself.

📍 *Great Northern Distillery Ltd.*
Carrick Road, Dundalk,
Co. Louth, +353 42 942 9005
↗ gndireland.com

Great Northern Distillery Ltd, Dundalk, Co. Louth

About 20 km away you will find the **Cooley Distillery** on the Cooley Peninsula, which was built close to the Cooley Mountains in County Louth in the 1980's by Dr. John Teeling. John Teeling was born in County Donegal. As a student, Dr. Teeling was forced by his university professor to give a lecture about the downfall of Irish whiskey. I'm sure he never dreamed that about 20 years later, he would become a pioneer of Irish whiskey and actively support the resurrection of the Irish whiskey industry. The distillery's location is ideal, as the river Slieve na gCloc passes directly by the building, making fresh water constantly available to the distillery. The Cooley distillery supported the old **Locke's Distillery** in Kilbeggan for a long time. Locke's Distillery is considered to be the oldest, continuously licensed whiskey distillery in the world and had to fight to stay open during the downturn of the whiskey industry and since 1970 was only kept afloat by a handful of people. Initially Locke's Distillery functioned as a museum, with the financial assistance of the Cooley Distillery. In 2007, exactly 54 years after it had ceased manufacturing, the distillery began to produce again. Nowadays Locke's Distillery sells up to 250,000 bottles of whiskey per year under the name Kilbeggan Distillery, and is therefore at the forefront of the revival of the traditional pot style distillation in Ireland. In 2013, John Teeling sold the Cooley Distillery to Jim Beam. The Cooley Distillery produces raw alcohol for all those that want to process, store, blend and sell it under their own name. The distillery currently offers the following brands: Greenore, Tyrconnell, Connemara and Kilbeggan Whiskeys. Both column style, as well as pot style are used. There are malt whiskeys (Tyrconnell), grain whiskeys (Kilbeggan, Greenore) and even a single malt whiskey (Connemara Peated), its smoky taste making it unique for Irish whiskey. Unfortunately, it is not possible to visit the Cooley Distillery as it is not open the public

📍 *Dundalk Road, Maddox Garden, Dundalk, Co. Louth*
+353 429376102, ↗ **kilbeggandistillingcompany.com**

COOLEY WHISKEY VISITOR CENTRE, MARTIN'S PUB & COOLEY WHISKEY BAR

Next to the distillery you will find an exhibition room in which you can see old tools that were used to produce poitín. You can also taste several whiskeys from the House of Cooley.

📍 *Dundalk Rd., Castecarragh, Dundalk, Co. Louth, +353 429376377*
↗ **cooleywhiskeybar.com**

In close proximity to the Cooley Distillery and Martin's Pub, there is an old mill from the 13th century. It's the home to **CARLINGFORD BREWING**. The brewer is guided by centuries old recipes, yet the produced beer is timeless. The brewery will give you an opportunity to taste the beer right there.

📍 *Carlingford Brewing*
The Old Mill, Dundalk
Road, Riverstown, A91 D850,
Co. Louth, +353 83 3284040
↗ **carlingfordbrewing.ie**

Carlingford Brewing, Co. Louth

The town of **CARLINGFORD** is situated at the top of the Cooley Peninsula between Carlingford Lough, a type of fjord that separates the Republic of Ireland and Northern Ireland, and the mountain Slieve Foye to the north east of Ireland. Carlingford is especially popular for its oyster farms. King John's Castle was built in the 12th century and has overlooked the harbour ever since. Also interesting is the Taaffe Castle, a tower like building from the 16th century. The Carlingford Heritage Centre, which you can find in a medieval church, offers you an overview of the local history. From here on you can decide whether to drive northwards, or head back to Dublin.

Carlingford Houber, Co. Louth

IRISH WHITETAIL DISTILLERY is an innovative family project by husband and wife team Nickolas and Violetta Boyls who are pioneering the patent pending Char Finishing process, whereby they are able to infuse a whiskey with the full flavour of a premium whiskey. This allows them to offer product at a mid-tier price, but provide premium flavoured products that can be enjoyed with any occassion. Char Finishing allows them to add new flavours and finishes to whiskey that was not previously possible. Once completed, the distillery will be family friendly and will encourage the exploration of the distillation process. through science in fun ways. Adult visitors will be able to experience multiple finishes of the same distillate and sample seasonal tastings making for a unique experience each time you visit. Please check on the website when the distillery open its doors to the public.

9 *Irish Whitetail Distillery*
↗ irishwhitetail.ie

THE KILKENNY TOUR

The Kilkenny Tour is a journey to the heart of Ireland. You will notice how the landscape changes continuously from plains to hills to small mountains. The route from Dublin brings you along the M7 and then you take the M9 in the direction of Kilkenny/Waterford.

ROYAL OAK DISTILLERY is a new, lesser known distillery which is situated in a beautiful location in the middle of Ireland. On your way to it you can enjoy perfect picture postcard views. The Walsh family had the idea to open a distillery in a place – as had been commonly done in the past – in the middle of the countryside and nestled in nature itself. When you reach Bagnalstown Royal Oak, you will be surrounded by barley and greeted by horses and cows. Even from a distance, if you look through the large windows of the distillery, you can admire the beauty of the three particularly long necked copper stills. The specialty in the production here is that during the distillation process the staff don't only rely on technology, but also on tests – smelling and tasting (palate), as well as visual tests which will determine the time when the next distillation step is introduced.

There are two whiskeys available: Writers' Tears and The Irishman. The name Writers' Tears is inspired by the great Irish authors like George Bernard Shaw, Oscar Wilde, W.B. Yeats, Lady Gregory, James Joyce, Samuel Beckett, Bram Stoker and others, who are known to have enjoyed whiskey in their time. Most of them lived in the 'Golden Whiskey Era' and fell for the amber coloured drink.

In 'Dubliners', Joyce wrote: 'The light music of whiskey falling into glasses made an agreeable interlude.' According to Samuel Becket, 'Whiskey bears a grudge against the decanter' – better in the glass in your hand than in the bottle on the shelf I reckon!

The Writers' Tears whiskeys are distilled with the pot still method while 'The Irishman' whiskeys come in three different types: The Irishman Single Malt, The Irishman 12 years and The Irishman Founders' Reserve, a blended whiskey.

The visitor centre is open the whole year round. The tour is very informative and the tour guide, Woody, who was present for the first hour of our tour, can answer any question you might have. There are also special events held here, for example on Valentine's Day or St. Patrick's Day –

Writters' Tears, Royal Oak Distillery Ltd, Royal Oak, Bagnalstown, Co. Carlow

celebrations with music and other surprises. An even bigger visitor centre is currently in the planning. This one will have its focus on life in the countryside and whiskey production during the 17th and 18th centuries.

♀ *Royal Oak Distillery Ltd, Royal Oak, Holloden House Demesne*
Clorusk Lower, Bagnalstown, R21 E086, Co. Carlow,
+353 59 913 32 32, ↗ walshwhiskey.com

KILKENNY is set in the heart of Ireland and has always been a centre of cultural trade. Kilkenny Castle was built in 1195 and you can still visit it today. The Dominican Black Abbey, and St. Canice's Cathedral were built in the 13th century, which makes Kilkenny a small town with a big history. Kilkenny claims to be the birth place of whiskey. I would not agree with that, however, it is true that the Bishop of Ledrede was the first to write down the manual on how to make 'aqua vitae' in the Red Book of the Diocese of Ossory

♀ *Kilkenny Castle, The Parade*
Collegepark, Kilkenny ,R95 YRK1,
+353 56 770 4100 ↗ kilkennycastel.ie
♀ *St. Canice's Cathedral, The Close, Coach Rd, Kilkenny*
R95 YRK1, +353 56 776 4971, ↗ stcanicescathedral.ie

Kilkenny Castle, Kilkenny Town, Co. Kilkenny

♀ *The Dominican Black Abbey, Abbey Sq, Abbey Street, Gardens, Kilkenny, R95 CD56, +353 567721279, ↗ dominicans.ie*

The Kilkenny Whiskey Guild is a network of ten pubs in Kilkenny, all of which offer whiskey events. You can take part in whiskey tastings offered by different producers. Especially interesting for Shem and I was to try the combination of whiskey and the offered food. The highlights were chocolate and whiskey, as well as goats' cheese and whiskey. You should not miss that! You will find the pubs and their offerings on the following website: ↗ **kilkennywhiskeyguild.com**

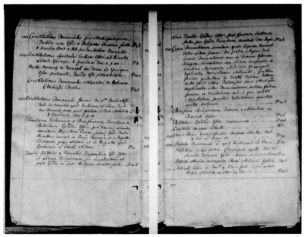

The Red Book of the Diocese of Ossory

Highbank Organic Farm is not a whiskey distillery, but an organic apple farm with a distillery. For apple lovers this is a must. Apart from their non-alcoholic products, they also produce gin, liquor brandy and apple

vodka. The farm is owned by the fifth generation of the Calder-Potts family who also reside there.

Here you will experience typical Irish hospitality. Take a tour around the farm on a hay wagon, visit the small but interesting distillery and admire the extraordinary pot still. Or you could simply test all the different products in their shop and if the weather permits it, sit outside and

Highbank Organic Farm, Cuffesgrange, Co. Kilkenny

take in the relaxed atmosphere with a nice view of the well-preserved old buildings. They also offer two beautiful rooms in case you taste so much that you need overnight accommodation.

📍 *Highbank Organic Farm, Cuffesgrange, R95 W58P*
Co. Kilkenny, +353 567729918
↗ highbankorchards.com

As we are already talking about traditional crafts, it is worth mentioning the **Jerpoint Glass Studio**. Since 1979 they have been using traditional glass blowing techniques to create beautiful art. There are not that many craftsmen who still master this technique.

📍 *Jerpoint Glass Studio, Glenmore, Stoneyford,*
R95 WN67, Co. Kilkenny, +353 56778 4350
↗ jerpointglass.com

Ballykeefe Distillery Ltd is a new, small, but lovely distillery located near Kilkenny. The distillery is situated on a farm and uses only home-made products and materials from the locality. As the distillery is not that big, only small amounts of whiskey are produced and as they only started the production recently, you will have to wait a little while longer to taste their first whiskey. In the meantime, you can try the gin made with 12 different ingredients, or the Irish Potato Vodka that has been distilled six times in pot stills. During the tour you can see the three copper pot stills, also with

Gin Pot Still , Testing Spirits in Ballykeefe Distillery

particularly long necks, which means the spirit comes in touch with a larger area of copper. Additionally, there is another pot still which is used only for gin production. It is a small, but beautifully functioning distillery and there is certainly a lot to see.

📍 *Ballykeefe Distillery Ltd., Kyle, Ballykeefe, Cuffsgrange, R95 NR50 Co. Kilkenny, +353 87 398 0088,* ↗ **ballykeefedistillery.ie**

Smithwick's is originally from Kilkenny and was founded there in the 16th century. It is one of the oldest breweries in Ireland. In the past it was part of the Franciscan Monastery. During the reformation, in 1537, the monasteries were dissolved and history stood still. Many years later, in 1705, two businessmen, John Smithwick and Richard Cole founded Smithwick's Kilkenny. The Smithwicks family sold the brewery in 1964 to Guinness and now, along with Guinness, it's owned by DIAGO. In 2014, the production was moved from Kilkenny to St. James' Gate brewery in Dublin, but you can still visit the old building and also taste the products there.

📍 *Smithwick's' Experience Kilkenny, 44 Parliament St., Gardens, Kilkenny, R95 VK54, Co. Kilkenny, +353 56 7786377* ↗ **smithwicksexperience.com.**

This could be a lovely relaxed two-day tour or just a day tour filled with great experiences. From here, you can either drive back to Dublin, continue to Cork (M8) or Waterford (M9) and after that, travel further in the direction of Midleton (more of that later).

WICKLOW

On this route you will find two whiskey distilleries with visitor centres. There's a pub with its own production and there's also a beer brewery. On top of that you can enjoy the beautiful landscape that inspired Tolkien to write about Hobbits and rings and things. For those who have more time on their hands, Wicklow offers ideal cycle tracks and hiking trails.

Lough Tay, also called Guinness Lake

Wicklow is a town as well as the name of the county. During this tour you can enjoy the **WICKLOW MOUNTAINS NATIONAL PARK** and the **SALLY GAP**. Fans of the television series 'Vikings' will especially appreciate the view of **LOUGH TAY**, also called Guinness Lake.

If you follow the M50 south (direction Wicklow/Wexford) on the N11 and exit at Number 7 (Bray/ Greystones), you will reach Kilruddery House. This estate was built in 1618 and has been the seat of the Earl of Meath for a long time. The house itself and the surrounding gardens can be visited. If you like, you can take a guided tour of the house and there is a farmers' market every Saturday.

📍 *Kilruddery House, Southern Cross, Bray, A98 W9F2, Co. Wicklow*
+353 01 2863405, ↗ kilruddery.com

If you continue from here on to Enniskerry, you'll find this pretty little village on the outskirts of Dublin. From there, just up the road a little is the **POWERSCOURT HOUSE & GARDENS**. Powerscourt is a Palladian mansion, built originally from a Norman castle in the 18th century. The estate with its landscaped gardens and breathtaking views over the Wicklow Mountains is one of the most beautiful sites of its kind in Ireland. On a warm sunny day there is nothing more appealing to me than to sit in their garden café and to simply enjoy the view. Approximately an hour's walk away is **POWERSCOURT WATERFALL**, the highest waterfall in Ireland where the River Dargle descends into the deep from a height of 90 to 130 metres. Here you can also find public barbecues to enjoy your own cooked meal. The estate, the park and the waterfall create a wonderful place to linger. Relax and enjoy the nature Ireland has to offer.

From December 2018, the **POWERSCOURT WHISKEY DISTILLERY** will be open to visitors. Just behind Powerscourt House at the end of the parking lot, you will find an old eighteenth century mill that now houses the new distillery and the storage rooms. The traditional pot stills can be seen from the windows as you walk towards the buildings. Not only do the new facilities

Powerscourt Whiskey Ltd

make a lovely impression, but so does the beautiful backdrop of the Wicklow Mountains.

The plan here is to produce both a single malt and pure pot still. Due to the similar names of both Powerscourt and Powers Whiskey and a possible resulting confusion, it was decided that the brand will be called Fercullen. They have branded it Fercullen14 year-old single malt and Fercullen 10 year-old. This was the original name of the area before it was changed to Powerscourt in 1618. From April on, you will be able to visit the facilities and enjoy their coffee and bar areas too.

📍 *Powerscourt Whiskey Ltd., Powerscourt Estate*
Powerscourt Distillery, Enniskerry, A98 W0D0, Co. Wicklow
↗ **powerscourtdistillery.com**

When you leave Powerscourt, should you decide to follow the signs for the Sally Gap, you'll be in for a treat. Sally Gap is a pass leading over the Wicklow Mountains. It was built after the Irish revolution in 1798, in order to enable the British army to chase the rebels. The landscape is a popular location for movie productions. Scenes for the movies 'P.S. I love you', 'Leap Year' and 'Harry Potter' have been filmed here.

Glendalough is situated at the end of the Sally Gap. **THE GLENDALOUGH MONASTIC SITE** is an early Christian monastic settlement. Today there are only ruins to be found, however, it is easy to envisage how the monks used to live. Nearby you can find the distillery of the same name.

♥ *Glendalough Monastic Site, Derrybawn, A98 TK71 Co. Wicklow*

↗ **glendalough.ie**

Glendalough Monastic Site, Co. Wicklow

The village of Glendalough almost joins seamlessly with the village of Laragh. Plans to bring the **GLENDALOUGH IRISH WHISKEY LTD.** company here are well under way. Currently Glendalough Irish Whiskey can be found in Newtownmountkennedy, which is 10km away and does not have its own visitor centre yet. This is planned to open in 2019 in Laragh, at the entrance to Glendalough village. As with many other small distilleries, it is not just whiskey which has been produced here since 2014, but also many other spirits. In earlier times, poitín was the main focus here. Especially interesting is their gin. For its production herbs from the Wicklow Mountains are used. The 'herb woman' ventures out into the mountains and collects what nature offers. Afterwards, the distiller brings out the best of these gifts of nature. I personally don't drink gin and while Shem doesn't favour gin, he could not get enough of the gin from the Glendalough distillery. The distillery offers different whiskeys, for example Glendalough 13 year-old Single Malt, Glendalough Double Barrel Single Grain, Single Malt, Glendalough 7 Year-Old Whiskey and Glendalough 13 year-old Mizunara Finish Single Malt.

♥ *Glendalough Irish Whiskey Ltd., Newtownmountkennedy, Co. Wicklow,* ↗ **glendaloughdistillery.com**

The Restaurant **WICKLOW HEATHER** is located only a stone's throw away from the Laragh distillery. If you happen to be hungry after a nice walk, I would definitely recommend to stop here. Next to the restaurant there is a whiskey bar and also the 'Writers Room', where you can find first editions of several Irish Authors' works.

📍 *Wicklow Heather, Glendalough Rd., Ballard, Laragh, A98 D983 Co. Wicklow, +353 404 45157,* ↗ **wicklowheather.ie**

Glenmalure is the next valley down to Glendalough and is an ideal hiking area. In the evening you can stop at the **GLENMALURE LODGE** to refresh yourself. In addition, there will most likely be live traditional Irish music. If you look at the address below, you will notice that it is difficult to find it in your navigation system. The place where the B&B is situated is called

Drumgoff. In case your navigation system can't find it, type in the name of the closest, larger village or town, for example Rathdrum or Glendalough in County Wicklow and find it this way. That is why it is so important to double check how to find the address either on your map or your smartphone. This applies in general when traveling around Ireland, not only to the Glenmalure Lodge.

📍 *Glenmalure Lodge, Drumgoff, Rathdrum, Glendalough, A67 WF65 Co. Wicklow, +353 404 46188,* ↗ **glenmalurelodge.ie**

Redcross is approximately 25 km away from Glenmalure. You can reach this village also by passing Avoca, where a visit to the old water mill and wool factory is highly recommended. The name Avoca might sound familiar to you as there is a chain store with Irish products that bears the same name. From Avoca, it is only 15 km to Redcross.

There you'll find the pub **O'DOMNAILL RUA'S** which in the past was a meeting point for travelers and an opportunity to exchange some gossip. The pub exists today pretty much as it was in the olden days and you can find their own brand whiskey on the shelves: 'Barr an Uisce'. Just like in the 18th century the pub still buys its whiskey from the Middleton distillery.

Before the alcohol is filled into bottles, water from the Avoca Valley is added. The river is in very close proximity to the pub, so is a useful source of water. The water is added in order to reduce the alcohol content. If you are in the area, do pay O'Domnaill Rua's a visit and try their whiskey, perhaps even to the sound of Irish music – a perfect combination.

📍 *Pub O'Domnaill Rua's*
Main Street, Redcross, A67 H799
Co. Wicklow, +353 404 4 1952
↗ **barranuisce.com**

Avoca Mill, Co. Wicklow

Just opposite the pub on the other side of the road, you'll find the **WICKLOW BREWERY** where you can try different craft beers. In the adjoining **MICKEY FINN'S PUB**, you can indulge in some pretty decent food and perhaps some music too. The area around Redcross is an ideal spot to take a break.

📍 *Mickey Finn's Pub*
Main Street, Redcross,
A67 H799, Co. Wicklow
+353 404 41661
↗ **wicklowbrewery.ie**

Mickey Finn's Pub

Also quite close is **Wicklow Town**. The town was named after the Vikings who chose the Wicklow bay as the perfect place for a base in the 9th century. Today you can visit the **Wicklow Gaol Museum** (an interesting historic jail), as well as the ruins of the **Black Castle**. In the harbour of Wicklow Town there is a special attraction too: a fish restaurant with a shop which is regularly visited by a seal. On the old coastal road, in the direction of Arklow, shortly after Wicklow Town, you will see three lighthouses. One of these originates from 1781 and can be rented as a guest-house. Even if you aren't intending to stay overnight there, it is a beautiful hiking trail.

📍 *Wicklow Head Lighthouse, Dunbur Head, Co. Wicklow,*
+353 1670 4733, ↗ **irishlandmark.com**

The area where the lighthouses are located is called **Dunbur** and therefore the **Wicklow Spirits Company Ltd.** named its product 'Dunbur Raspberry Infusion Irish Whiskey Liqueur' – try asking for one of those after you've had a few too many! The German who jointly owns it is Heike Owens and she says she was inspired by the spectacular surrounding of the 'Dunbur Head', the most eastern point in Ireland. The '**Dunbur Head**' is, with its impressive lighthouses and the magnificent views along the east coast of Ireland, a truly unique place. The liqueur is made out of Irish whiskey, berries and honey. It is a unique creation which gives this drink a fruity-sweet note and a glowing ruby red colour. You can also purchase this liqueur through various online suppliers.

Wicklow Harbour, Co. Wicklow

From here on you can drive back to Dublin along the coastline. In doing so you might stop in Greystones or Bray before you get back to the city. Alternatively, you could just keep on driving south in the direction of Wexford, Waterford or even Cork.

"Whisky is liquid sunshine."
George Bernard Shaw

A Trip from the East of the Island to the West

If you cross Ireland from east to west, you will encounter two places that play a hugely important role in the history of whiskey and it's almost a must to visit them. If you only have one day available, you should go to the town of Tullamore or Kilbeggan and have a nice day trip. For those who have more time on their hands, I recommend driving to Galway and from there, visiting the Cliffs of Moher in nearby Co. Clare or the Connemara National park.

Shem is not the biggest fan of the drive from Dublin to Galway as he finds it boring to spend so much time on the motorway. I on the other hand, find this route especially handy and easy for motorists that are not used to driving on the left.

The tour from Dublin to Galway is not that long, but leads through several different counties, hence you will be continuously greeted by friendly signs along the way, warmly welcoming you to whichever county you are entering. Keep an eye out for the artwork that is displayed along the motorway. My favourite is a bull being pulled across the road by a farmer – don't worry, so far the farmer hasn't succeeded in moving him an inch, so it's unlikely to impede your progress. In my opinion, it's one of the best artistic pieces, but feel free to find your own favourite motorway artwork.

Your journey will lead you from the Dublin Ring Road (M50) on to the M4 in the direction of Galway. Shortly after you leave the M50 and if you want to venture off the motorway, you could pay a visit to the small town of Celbridge, situated in county Kildare. There you can view **CASTLETOWN HOUSE**, the largest and most significant country house in Ireland. It was built in the Palladian style – meaning it was inspired by the Italian architect Andrea Palladio. Born more than 500 years ago, Palladio is considered to be among the world's most influential architects.

An excursion to this place offers the perfect possibility for those who not only want to experience the city of Dublin, but also would like to see some nature. The trip is an easy one and you can even take a bus to Celbridge.

Castletown House was built in 1722 for the Irish President of Parliament, William Connolly (1662–1729). Designs from several prominent architects were used. Among those were Alessandro Galilei, Sir Edward Lovett Pearce and later Sir William Chambers.

In 1965, the whole estate was sold by the Connolly-Carew family to a building constructor. In 1967, Congressman Desmond Guinness, a founder of the Irish Georgian Society, purchased the house and a part of the park area.

Guinness, along with the Castletown Foundation who bought the house in 1979, felt an obligation to preserve the building. The challenging

Castletown House, Celbridge, Co. Kildare

restoration of the main chambers demanded great effort and financial resources. Eventually, on the 1st January 1994, Castletown House was taken over by the Irish state.

It is worth taking a look at the events calendar on the house's website as there is a great choice of activities available there and something for everybody to enjoy. If you like picnics, Castletown is also an ideal destination.

♥ *Castletown House, W23 V9H3, County Kildare*
+353 16288383, ⌐ castletown.ie

From here you can continue following the M4 in the direction of Galway. At Kinnegad the M4 divides and you take the M6. After approximately 20 minutes you will reach Kilbeggan. Kilbeggan is situated in County Westmeath, at the shores of the River Brosna and is bedded into the hills of Esker Riada, an accumulation of basal hills (Eskers) made of sand, gravel and errant blocks. These extend from Kilbeggan to Tyrellspass. At first Kilbeggan appears to be a sleepy town, it is, however, the home of one of the very few cooperages in Ireland. It's also the home of the Kilbeggan Whiskey distillery (Locke's Distillery).

Cooperage, Kilbeggan, Co. Westmeath

The **WORKING COOPERAGE** is located in the town centre and accessible to visitors. John Neilly, one of the last coopers in Ireland works there. The making of barrels has a long-standing tradition in his family. John now owns the last remaining free cooperage in Ireland and mainly works for the new distillery 'Nephin' in Co. Mayo. You can watch him in the Cooperage, repairing or toasting barrels. Visitors looking for some guidance on their career path will have the ideal opportunity to act as an apprentice in one of the oldest professions in the world. It is advisable to have plenty of time, as with many Irish, John also loves to tell stories. Shem and I really enjoyed our time with him. The working cooperage is next to the Kilbeggan Distillery.

📍 *Nephin Cooperage, Relic Rd., Kilbeggan N91 CY54, Co. Westmeath*
Opening Hours 10am–16pm, lunch break 13-14 pm
↗ **facebook.com/john.neilly.33**

The **KILBEGGAN DISTILLERY**, also known by the name Locke's Distillery, is located on the Main Street of Kilbeggan. The Kilbeggan Distillery has been fighting for a long time with Bushmills about who the title 'oldest distillery in Ireland' belongs to. If you look at the founding year, the Kilbeggan distillery is in the better position, as it was founded already in 1757, however, from 1957 onwards it was closed for 54 years, therefore

Visitor Centre Kilbeggan Distillery Experience, Kilbeggan

Bushmills actually is ahead in terms of operation period. Just another little dispute around the topic of whiskey, where we will never have a clear winner.

As already mentioned, the Kilbeggan distillery was closed from 1957 onwards. In 2007, the Cooley distillery reopened it by using the warehouses in Kilbeggan to store their whiskey. For the 250th anniversary of the Kilbeggan distillery, the 'Locke's distillery museum' was opened there. It is definitely worth a visit, as you probably won't get the opportunity anytime soon again to get an insight into such an old distillery. One of the old copper stills, last used in the 19th century, has been

Visitor Centre Kilbeggan Distillery Experience, Kilbeggan

carefully restored and on the 19th March 2007 was lit again – exactly 54 years to the day since production had stopped. Therefore, this copper still is currently the oldest one in use in Ireland. By bringing it back into service, the old traditional style of whiskey making in Ireland has been revived and respect paid to the craftsmen of long ago.

Today the Kilbeggan distillery produces up to 250,000 bottles of whiskey per year, all of which is maturing in the adjoining granite halls. For Shem and I, the special thing about this distillery is the fact that you can view the old equipment and crushing mill. If you have visited modern whiskey distilleries before, you can easily compare how little, and what exactly has changed during the last 400 years of whiskey production.

The Kilbeggan distillery offers the following brands: Greenore, Tyrconnell, Connemara and Kilbeggan Whiskeys. For the distillation process both the column still as well as the pot still are used. There are malt whiskeys (Tyrconnell), grain whiskeys (Kilbeggan, Greenore) and even a single malt peated whiskey (Connemara Peated).

♥ *Visitor Centre Kilbeggan Distillery Experience, Lower Main St.* *Kilbeggan, N91 K79Y, Co. Westmeath, +353 57 9332134* ↗ **kilbeggandistillery.com.**

Approximately 10 kilometres from Kilbeggan is **TULLAMORE**, a much larger town in the County of Offaly. From there you can do excursions into

Tullamore D.E.W. Old Bonded Warehouse, Tullamore, Co. Offaly

the nearby Slieve Bloom Mountains. Although the highest hill is only 500 metres above sea level, this place offers many hiking trails, cycle tracks and picnic areas with beautiful views of the surrounding countryside. The Grand Canal passes through Tullamore and connects Dublin in the east with the River Shannon in the west of Ireland. In the past, the Grand Canal was the most important transportation route for goods.

Tullamore D.E.W. Old Bonded Warehouse, Co. Offaly

In former times, the **TULLAMORE WHISKEY DISTILLERY**, founded by Michael Molloy in 1829, was directly positioned by the Grand Canal. The whiskey and distillery name 'Tullamore DEW' was made up by Molloy's nephew. 'DEW' stands for the initials Daniel E. Williams, who modernised and managed the distillery successfully.

In the 1960's, he cleverly positioned the distillery on the market for the future. He is also the creator of the slogan 'Give every man his DEW'. In Alfred Barnard's book from 1886, he mentioned that the warehouses alone extended over an area of four hectares. Furthermore, there were eight granaries, four baking ovens to dry the barley, four malt houses and a mill house with eight millstones. Unfortunately, from 1920 onwards, Tullamore like most distilleries, also had to fight to stay afloat. In the hope of better times, a support unit for the column still procedure was constructed. As this measure didn't bring the longed-for boom, the distillery looked to an old drink from the 17th century. It consisted of whiskey, herbs and honey. This lifeline came from Austria, where somebody was able to retrieve an old recipe from his ancestors. With this recipe, formerly called 'heather wine', the drink 'Irish Mist' was born.

In 1954 and after 125 years, the distillery had to close its doors. In 1960, the then owner, successfully revived the brand and sold it to 'Irish Distillers'. In 1994, the brand 'Tullamore' was sold to the C&C group, the production, however, remained in Midleton. In 2010, William Grant and Sons purchased the brand name and in 2014, they brought it home to Tullamore. The new distillery now produces 'Single Malt' and 'Pot Still Whiskey'. They still use ingredients from Midleton for several blended whiskeys. On the grounds of the former Tullamore DEW distillery, directly by the canal, in a former customs warehouse, you'll find the D.E.W. Heritage Centre. In this visitor centre you will receive an overview of the whiskey manufacturing process, the history of the distillery and the types of whiskeys that were produced – or are still in production here. During the tour you will be given insights into the secrets about the origin of the ingredients, as well as old and new manufacturing methods. During the whiskey tasting at

Pot Stills, Tullamore D.E.W. Old Bonded Warehouse

the end of the tour, Shem and I found 'our DEW'. We would also recommend the restaurant area where you can enjoy your whiskey or the tasty meals outside next to the canal. The Tullamore DEW itself is a combination of several matured whiskeys.

Tullamore D.E.W. offer the following whiskeys: 10-year-old Single Malt Blended whiskeys with a high ration of pot still, 12-year-old Special Reserve, 15-year-old Trilogy Small Batch and Phoenix, a triple distilled whiskey made of a mixture of grain, malt and pot still whiskey. For liqueur fans I'd recommend Irish Mist which is still made using the old traditional recipe even to this day.

📍 *Tullamore D.E.W. Old Bonded Warehouse, Bury Quay, Puttaghan Tullamore, R35 Y5V0, Co. Offaly, +353 57 932 5015*
↗ tullamoredew.com

We continue on the motorway in the direction of Galway. Those of you who are not under time pressure and interested in the Celts should definitely visit **CLONMACNOISE**. This is an early Christian monastery which was founded in the middle of the 16th century by Irish Saint Ciaran on the east riverbank of the Shannon. The site includes the ruins of a cathedral, seven churches from the 10th to the 13th centuries, two round towers, three high crosses and the largest collection of early Christian tomb slabs in Western Europe. The original high crosses and tomb slabs are displayed in the visitor centre. The long and varied history of

Clonmacnoise Monastery, Shannonbridge, Co. Offaly

Clonmacnoise is presented during an audio visual tour in the visitor centre. Furthermore, there a several exhibition rooms dedicated to the wildlife and landscapes of this region.

📍 *Clonmacnoise, Shannonbridge, Athlone, N37 V292, Co. Offaly, +353 90 967 4195,*
↗ heritageireland.ie/en/midlands-eastcoast/clonmacnoise/

You now have a choice. You can either drive back onto the motorway or take the country roads and drive to the small town of **SHANNONBRIDGE**. Shannonbridge is situated directly at the shores of the River Shannon and at the border between counties Offaly and Roscommon. Its name originates from the fascinating bridge built in 1757 and which divides the village in two. You can also still see old fortifications and ruins from the era of the Napoleonic wars. The most fascinating landmarks in Shannonbridge for Shem and I, however, are two outstanding pubs.

One is **J.J. KILLEEN'S VILLAGE TAVERN**. It's a really cosy traditional Irish pub, full of charm and class. You wouldn't think so, but this kind of pub unfortunately belongs to a dying species in the modern world. It is located in a 350-year-old house. The pub and the adjoining shop have been in the same family for over 80 years and

Killeen's Village Tavern, Raghra, Shannonbridge

in all this time, very little has been changed. Killeen's Village Tavern consists of a pub, a little shop and a bistro/restaurant area. In the little shop you can actually find everything you need – everything including the kitchen sink! In the evening the shop counter transforms into a bar counter at which Shem and I love to sit and relax. The immensely welcoming natives are excited to share a friendly conversation with visitors. And of course, having the 'Craic' is an every day theme here.

📍 *Killeen's Village Tavern, Raghra, Shannonbridge, N37 K7T8*
Co. Offaly, +353 90 967 4112, ↗ *killeens.ie*

Luker's Pub, Shannonbridge

The second pub, Luker's Pub, can be found directly at the bridge. The new area with its big windows and a lovely view onto the river, is very inviting. The most interesting thing, however, is that the original pub managed to keep its old world charm intact by looking exactly like it did 60 years ago. As if time had frozen it. The shop is located in the front area and in another part is the pub with an open fire. This is a truly interesting piece of history found in the middle of Shannonbridge.

📍 *Luker's Pub, Restaurant & Live Music Venue, Main St., Raghra,*
Shannonbridge, N37 XK75, Co. Offaly, +353 90 967 4995
↗ *lukersbar.com*

Another tip is the restaurant which recently opened called **THE OLD FORT**. It's on the other side of the river – across from Luker's and from the first floor you can enjoy the magnificent view over the Shannon and the old arched bridge.

The Old Fort , Shannonbridge, Co. Offaly

📍 *The Old Fort, Raghrabeg, Shannonbridge, N37 XT54, Co. Offaly*
+353 909674973, ↗ **the-old-fort-restaurant.business.site**

On the way back to the motorway, in the direction of Galway, you will follow the R357. This route passes by the town of **ATHLONE**, which is situated in the centre of Ireland. Because of its location, Athlone was an important military base for a long time. The well-positioned fort is a reminder of this time. You can visit the medieval castle in the town centre, which hosts an exhibition about the town and its history. You will also get a beautiful view over the city and the River Shannon.

Since 1740 whiskey has been produced in Athlone. In total 38 distilleries and breweries were known of. As Athlone is on the River Shannon, the distilleries had better access to water and barley. Because of the River Shannon and the

River Shannon in Athlone, Co. Westmeath

Royal Canal, the connections to Dublin, Galway and Cork were very good and the finished product could be transported cost effectively.

Unfortunately, there is not much left to see of the buildings of the former 'Whiskey Boom' era, nevertheless, it was interesting to explore the town during the **'ATHLONE WHISKEY WALKING TOUR'**. Not only did we walk, we also made a pit stop to eat chocolate and drink whiskey. We enjoyed a chat with the owner of a 900 year old pub and were allowed to try his whiskey. It's simply called Sean's Bar and is also known widely for its music. These were three hours very well spent.

Sean's Bar, Athlone, Co. Westmeath

At the river bank there is a company offering boat tours. The **'VIKING TOUR'** will bring you on a perfectly reconstructed Viking ship over the River Shannon to Lough Ree lake or to Clonmacnois, the old monastery settlement mentioned earlier.

Athlone Whiskey Walking Tours, +353 85 2380023
↗ *athlonewhiskeytours.ie*
📍 *Viking Tours Ireland, The Quay, Athlone, Co. Westmeath*
+353 862621136

The city of **GALWAY** was founded in 1124 and is situated on the west coast of Ireland. It is not a big city, but it certainly has a very vibrant centre. There are the characteristic Georgian houses with their colourful doorways and old shop signs which were typical in the 19th century. For Shem, Galway is especially known for its big annual horse racing week, the Galway Races.

Galway City, Co. Galway

After Dublin transformed itself more and more into a commercial capital, a lot of artists were drawn to Galway. Many came to visit and never left. Galway is well known for its art and music scene. The centre has an abundance of brightly coloured front doors, Victorian architecture and more than its fair share of traditional pubs – a typically Irish town – and then some! For more information please visit ↗ **galwaytourism.ie**

As expected, Galway also has its part in the history of the Irish whiskey industry. The **'PERSSE GALWAY WHISKEY DISTILLERY'** (H.S. Persse Nun's Island Distillery) manufactured from 1815 until approximately 1913. Through historical events, Galway has a very strong connection to Spain. Many Spanish businessmen settled down in Galway and even the layout of the city is very similar to a Spanish town. Despite a past influenced by wine and spirit trade, **NUN'S ISLAND DISTILLERY** was the only legal distillery that was operated in the second half the 19th century in Connaught. The distillery was located right on the River Corrib and was run by the Persse family, who were great supporters of this region as well as the arts. Lady Gregory for example, the grandniece of Henry Stafford Persse, was born as Isabella Augusta Persse. George Bernard Shaw referred to her as the 'greatest living Irishwoman' due to her great dedication to Irish literature.

For 2018, the family is planning to bring a 'Persse Galway Whiskey' to the market. The Persse's Galway whiskey is said to follow the example of the other fine Irish whiskeys on the market and to serve as a reminder of

Galway City, Co. Galway

the history of Galway and the Persse family. Unfortunately, I was not able to taste the whiskey at the time of writing, but very much look forward to it and believe that it will be a soft and mild whiskey giving a taste of history. ↗ perssesgalwaywhiskey.ie

Galway is also the origin of the **CLADDAGH RING**. The ring is at the centre of a nice Irish tradition that's still around today. The ring shows a heart with a crown that is held by two hands and is usually given to a

loved one. Originally, this traditional ring was made in the small village of Claddagh, which is situated at the edge of Galway City. The hands of the ring symbolise friendship, the heart symbolises love and the crown loyalty. While it's been around since the seventeenth century, it's still worn by many today and especially popular for men to wear as a wedding band. The way the ring is worn will show you if the person who wears it is married, widowed, engaged or looking for a partner. As you can see this ring will give you a lot of information if you are on the lookout for some romance!

♥ *Claddagh Arts Centre and Katies Claddagh Cottage Fairhill Rd. Upper, The Claddagh, H91 ERW5, Co. Galway +353 87828 0848,* ↗ *claddaghdesigns.ie/*

The Galway pubs specialising in Irish whiskey have published a map which provides an overview of the local traditional Irish pubs and the different types of whiskey ↗ galwaywhiskeytrail.ie

PADRAIC O'GRIALLAIS is a new poitín distillery in County Galway. The owners are the fifth generation producing poitín. The grandfather of the current owner passed on his secrets about its production to the next generations. You should try the delicious 'Micil Irish Poitín'. Unfortunately, the distillery does not have a visitor centre, however, you can take part in several whiskey tastings. For appointments please refer to their webpage.

♥ *Padraic O'Griallais, Lochan Beag, Co. Galway* ↗ micilpoitin.com

Aran Islands, Galway Bay, Co. Galway

County Galway is a region where Irish is still spoken frequently. The further you travel out of Galway, the higher the probability that you will meet people who speak English with you, but talk Irish among themselves. Here, you'll also find a lot of Irish music and also Irish dancing in

Connemara National Park, County Galway

the pubs. We experienced this in a pub and B&B called **'Pádraicíns'** in the village of Furbo.

📍 *'An Cheibh Bar', Rossaveal, Co.Galway, +353 877857797*
↗ **charterireland.ie**

The next beautifullandmark which is well worth a visit is Kylemore Abbey, a Benedictine monastery founded in 1920 in the grounds of Kylemore Castle. There you will also find a small shop and a tea house where you can take a tasty break. Nature lovers will be amazed by the Victorian Walled Garden and the Oak Plantation. Or you could just take some time out and go for a walk through the woods. With its Gothic church, Kylemore Abbey and the mausoleum are places that are also architecturally very interesting. All in all, it is a magical place to relax and unwind.

📍 *Kylemore Abbey, Kylemore, Pollacappul, Connemara, H91 VR90*
Co. Galway, +353 95 41146, ↗ **kylemoreabbey.com**

In the following web sites you will find an overview of some other places of interest:

📍 *Irish marble Gemstones of Ireland, Moycullen, Co. Galway,*
+353 55 5102, ↗ **connemaramarble.ie**
Cliffs of Moher Cruises, +353 65707 5949,
↗ **doolin2aranferries.com**
Cliffs of Moher Cruises, +353 65 707 5555,
↗ **doolinferry.com**
Charter Ireland, +353 87 785 7731,
↗ **charterireland.ie**

From here on, you can continue along the Atlantic coast to either the north or the south. If you are searching for further travel inspirations, you should look for routes in the direction of Dingle/Kerry or alternatively the 'North tour/West coast'. Either will prove to be a good choice.

Let's go north!

As previously mentioned, Ireland has been divided into two parts since 1916 – on the one hand the Republic of Ireland and on the other hand, Northern Ireland. Northern Ireland is under the rule of Great Britain. If we are talking about 'the North', this can often lead to confusion as County Donegal, which belongs to the Republic of Ireland, is situated in the northwest of the Irish island. The Irish generally talk about 'the North', as they consider both Donegal and the six counties as one geographical unit. Interestingly, while being a part of the Irish Republic and therefore one of the twenty six counties, Donegal shares less than ten kilometers of border with the republic. In Donegal I've heard it said that you have the six counties, the twenty five counties and then you have Donegal.

Because of the fact that Northern Ireland is ruled by Great Britain, its official currency is the Pound Sterling and the road signs comply with those of Great Britain, i.e. miles per hour rather than kilometers, as used in Ireland and the rest of Europe. You will also have to change the country in your navigation system to Northern Ireland, as it will not know that you are not in the Republic of Ireland anymore. Although border checkpoints do not exist anymore, you should check beforehand in case you need a visa for Northern

Ireland. At the moment it's quite unclear as to what impact Brexit will have on the situation – there will be interesting times ahead. I think it would be advisable therefore, to inform yourself before you start your trip.

While nowadays it is not a problem driving from one country to the next, the same cannot be said of the relatively recent Irish political history and I couldn't help noticing Shem's change from his usual calm and relaxed manner. In some places I would notice him becoming tense and stressed. This is due to the fact that up to about 10 years ago it was not always safe to drive around Northern Ireland in a car with an Irish number plate.

Basically, it is safe to travel in Northern Ireland. There are three days in the year where demonstrations take place, but usually life continues as normal. I won't sugar coat anything, there were two days I was there where the police and some of the military were on the streets and I felt a bit uncomfortable. That being said, it is a rare occurrence. The dates in question were 12th July, 5th August and Easter Sunday (politically difficult days in Northern Ireland).

After the Easter Rising in 1916 and many years of unrest before that, the treaty eventually signed contained an agreement that a part of the Northern Irish island, the six counties, would remain under British rule. This was based on the argument that mostly protestants lived there and therefore these people would identify as British. This fact wasn't quite true, as the af-

Carnfunnock Country Park, Drains Bay and Ballygally, near Larne, County Antrim

fected territory was home to both Protestants and Catholics. The decision to divide the north of Ireland into the Republic of Ireland and the United Kingdom lead to the sudden partition of streets, city parts and villages, depending on the majority religion that was represented in that particular area. You will notice this on the streets of the villages, towns and cities. In areas which are predominantly Catholic, road signs are written in English and Irish like in the Republic, some even include the Irish flag, as the Catholics generally identify with the Irish. With the Protestants, often referred to as Royalists, you will find the British flag everywhere you go. In Belfast, even the kerbstones are marked with the respective colours, so that nobody runs into danger and ends up in the wrong part of town.

Carlingford Town, Cooley Peninsula, County Louth

While I was booking the B&Bs for our tour, I rarely paid attention to this aspect of Irish history. My main focus was to find accommodation close to the relevant whiskey distilleries. I wasn't aware at all that in doing so, I was bringing Shem into stressful situations. As already mentioned, most addresses only consist of the name of the place and the county. This was also the case here in the North, so that we often had to call the B&Bs and ask for more detailed directions while on the road as we were not able to find them. During our searches Shem often found himself surrounded by British flags and told me nervously that we, and the car, would not be safe in this area. I thought he was exaggerating. Who would attack us in this cute little village in the middle of the mountains? Once we parked our car in a car park and noticed four men drinking beer and relaxing outside in the sun. Shem explained to me again that neither we nor the car would be safe here and we would have trouble with these men. Normally Shem is the most relaxed person and I hadn't ever seen him in such a state of panic before. Just to play it safe I reached for my mobile and pretended to make a call in German to make it clear to them that I was not Irish. Then we went for a nice meal and had a drink in the pub to calm our nerves. The natives in the pub even bought us a round of whiskey. An Irish friend told me afterwards that such a warm welcome is quite common nowadays. Before we left I inspected the car to make sure no damage had been done to it and we then settled into our rooms. The car was fine, however, I have to say that Shem was right about the fact that there would be trouble with the four men. But it was trouble of a very different kind from that which Shem had anticipated. The men were in fact foreign construction workers on a day off for the first time in weeks and therefore enjoying a good few drinks in their room and were more than noisy as a result.

On my return home I spoke to a friend about my experience and she also confirmed that she has never had a bad experience in the North, but despite this she is as anxious as Shem when traveling there.

You can start with our North Tour from the outskirts of Dublin. If you revisit the chapter 'Short trips around Dublin', you will find the **SLANE TOUR** and the **COOLEY PENINSULA TOUR**.

If you have decided to do the Slane Tour you can continue on the N2 northbound, where you can stop in the little town of Derrylavan. Here you will find the **OLD CARRICK MILL DISTILLERY**. At the moment they only produce gin, but they did announce in 2017 that they will soon begin to produce whiskey which will be matured in French Bordeaux barrels. Like me, you might ask yourself how they got that idea. As we found out, this mill was run by the ancestors of the excellent winemaker 'Barton and Guestier' in the 18th century. Locally, the mill is still called 'Barton's

Old Carrick Mill Distillery, Co. Monaghan

Mill'. The idea came about at a trade fair in Florida when both companies decided to cooperate. The French winemakers delivered 50 used 350-litre barrels made of French oak to the distillery, barrels which had been previously used to mature Chateau Magnol. A limited edition of 'Founder's Reserve' whiskey will be matured in these barrels. The plan is to restore the old mill to a standard where even barley can be ground again. A visitor centre is also in the planning. Due to the fact that there is no reliable schedule for this project, you should consult the website to see how far along the plans are before paying a visit.

♥ *Old Carrick Mill Distillery, Derrylavan, A81 CY28, Co. Monaghan +353 87 103 4890, ↗ oldcarrick.ie*

Sun Set, Portaferry, County Down, Northern Ireland

If you are coming directly from Dublin, or if you do a detour on your trip, you should definitely go back onto the M1/N1. Once you have reached the town of Newry, you are already in Northern Ireland. As previously mentioned, I have arranged the route in a way that the order of the stops are logical. From Newry you can drive directly to Belfast, or you can choose to go in the direction of Sligo and Donegal. We will head in the direction of the Ards Pensinsula, which can be reached either from the north towards Belfast/Bangor or with the ferry from Strangford to Portaferry. The Ards Peninsula (from Irish Aird Uladh, meaning 'peninsula of the Ulstermen') is surrounded by water on three sides. In the small town of Portavogie you will find yourself at the most easterly point of Ireland.

The peninsula was conquered in the 12th century by the Normans and became a place of significance due to its castles and churches. During the Second World War the peninsula and surrounding areas were utilised for landing strips by the allied air forces. You can still find neat pieces of history detailing this in nearby Kirkistown.

On the Ards Pensinsula you will encounter a real jewel of a distillery, namely the **ECHLINVILLE DISTILLERY**. The current managing director, Shane Braniff, built a new distillery next to the old building which originates from 1730. In the remaining buildings, he is planning a type of 'academy' for those visitors who would like to experience more than just a whiskey tasting. The old barns will be the accommodation and workshops for the future students. The distillery already has a wide variety of products in its range, despite the fact that this is a very young distillery, only producing whiskey since 2016. The old whisky brand 'Dunville' from Belfast found its new home in the Echlinville Distillery after an 80 year break. **THE DUNVILLE & CO., ROYAL IRISH DISTILLERY** was founded in 1868 as a family business in Belfast, but had to cease production in 1938.

The Echlinville Distillery is also a family business. Shane Braniff places great value in selecting ingredients that are sourced locally. That is why he only uses home grown barley. This grows very well in the special maritime climate of the peninsula. Due to the fact that the distillery is not easily reachable, you should book your tour online in advance. Once on site, you can enjoy the famous Irish hospitality to the full. Be prepared to spend a little bit more time here, especially if Shane Braniff guides your tour – his tours are full of exciting stories about whiskey and whiskey production in Ireland. As he has so much to tell you, he always takes a little longer for the tour than might be advertised.

Echlinville Distillery, Newtownards, Co. Down

On the grounds of Echlinville Distillery there is also a vehicle museum. This collection of old cars and motorcycles is a second passion of Shane's. The collection also showcases some military vehicles, namely four tanks alongside the cars, including some old versions of the original Mini.

♀ *Echlinville Distillery, Echlinville House, 62 Gransha Rd., Newtownards BT22 1AJ, Co. Down, +44 2842738597*
↗ echlinville.com

Perhaps there are people among you who are, like Shem, fans of high speed. The motor racing track will give the opportunity to this not-so-rare species, not only to watch others racing, but also to do a few fast laps and imagine they are racing drivers too.

♀ *Motor Racing Track, 130 Rubane Rd., Kircubbin, Newtownards BT22 1AU, UK, +44 28 4277 1325,* ↗ kirkistown.com

The town of **BANGOR** is situated right up in the north of the Island. It has its origins in the Bronze Age, when the Vikings attacked the island. Today, it is a modern town with well preserved historical sites, for example Bangor Abbey or the historical castle. If you don't want to drive by car to Belfast, you can use the train service. It is hard to say goodbye to this beautiful peninsula, but our adventure doesn't end here, we are off to Belfast.

Rail Bridge, Co. Armagh, NI

Parliament Buildings, Belfast

BELFAST

Belfast has always been an industrial city. Although the scars that remain after the fighting between Catholics and Protestants are still visible, Belfast is now a vibrant city, offering a wide range of interesting places to see. While you are visiting, please bear in mind that there are still certain days where demonstrations take place, for example during the week of the 12th July with the 'Orange March'. It happened once, that I found myself caught up in such a demonstration and I can assure you it was not a nice experience. The police were present in high numbers, which led to a feeling of insecurity rather than one of reassurance. In the end nothing happened, but the presence of so many armed police men gave me the impression that something could happen at any time. During the Hop on Hop off bus tour we received a good overview of the sights, the city, the people and the changes that have taken place over the last 20 years. Shem was particularly interested in the changes and in the places that he had seen in the horrific news stories of the past. We also did a walking tour with our tour guide Denis. He gave us his account of the 'Whiskey history' of Belfast. During the heyday of the whiskey era, there were

Albert Memorial Clock, Belfast

several whiskey distilleries in Belfast. **AVONIEL DISTILLERY, RAVENHILL ROAD** and **CROMAC DISTILLERY** based in Corporation Street were among the most important ones. The largest distillery, however, was Dunville's with its production of more than 2.5 million gallons per year (a British gallon corresponds to 4.55 liters).

In 1899, there were 18 distilleries and several whiskey dealers registered in Belfast. To manufacture their 'homegrown' whiskey, the distilleries used water from Lough Mourne, a lake situated approximately 12 miles from most of the distilleries.

📍 *Denis Traveler Guide +44 79 4425 6560*
↗ belfastcompasstours.com

As stated previously, the **DUNVILLE & CO., ROYAL IRISH DISTILLERY** was the distillery that produced the most whiskey in Belfast back then. It was founded in 1825, though by 1938 it had closed again. In 1837, Dunville presented their first pot still whiskey, therefore it does not lack in tradition. Up to 1930

Old headquarters, Dunville Whiskey Distillery, Belfast

it was a purely family-owned business, but unfortunately it was missing proper leadership, which might otherwise have saved the distillery during the hard times. Fortunately, in my opinion, the old name was saved by the Echlinville Distillery. Even today, you can find old advertisements for Dunville's, for example on mirrors or metal signs. The only historical buildings remaining are the company headquarters and the assembly room of Dunville's. Nowadays you'll find a bar and restaurant there.

The **BELFAST DISTILLERY COMPANY** will be opened shortly. Peter Lavery, a bus driver in a previous life, won the lottery and used his winnings to fulfil his dream of having his own whiskey distillery. In true style, he chose a former prison building to house his new distillery. Currently Lavery's whiskey is produced in the Cooley distillery. It is not yet clear when the business will move and when the visitor centre will open its doors.

📍 *Belfast Distillery Company, Crumlin Road Gaol 53–55 Crumlin Rd, Belfast, Antrim, BT14 6ST,* ↗ belfastdc.com

Duke of York, Belfast *Dark Horse Pub, Belfast*

DARK HORSE is a pub which stocks an excellent variety of Irish whiskeys. Every inch of the pub is decorated with traditional advertisements (mirrors and metal signs) from Irish distilleries who are both still in business and closed down. The **DUKE OF YORK** offers tasty food and a broad range of whiskeys. The pub is situated in an old Victorian style. Both of these pubs are well worth a visit and can be found in Belfast, located along narrow alleyways in the city centre.

♥ Dark Horse Pub, Hill St. Belfast BT1 2LB, UK, 44 28 90241062
♥ Duke of York, 7-11 Commercial Court, Belfast, BT1 2NB
+44 2890241062, ↗ **dukeofyorkbelfast.com**

The Crown Liquor Saloon, also known as the **CROWN BAR**, is a pub in Great Victoria Street in Belfast. Refurbished in 1885 and at least twice since, it is an outstanding example of a Victorian gin palace and one of Northern Ireland's best-known pubs. It is owned by the National Trust.

♥ The Crown Bar
Liquor Saloon
46 Great Victoria St.
Belfast BT2 7 BA, NI
+44 28 9024 3187
↗ **nicholsonspubs.co.uk**

Ballintoy next to Carrick-a-Rede Rope Bridge, County Antrim, Northern Ireland

From Belfast, you can drive directly to Bushmills if you like. Take the M2, then switch to the A26, which will lead you straight there. Otherwise, you could take a small detour, which for nature lovers is an absolute must. For this you have to drive on the A44 in the direction of Killagan Bridge/ Ballycastle and follow the signs for **CARRICK-A-REDE ROPE BRIDGE** and the **GIANT'S CAUSEWAY**. For each of the aforementioned landmarks, you should plan at least half a day. Both the Carrick-a-Rede Rope Bridge and the Giant's Causeway offer breathtaking views. With a little luck the sea will be a beautiful turquoise colour. The colour was so extraordinary that people that have seen our photos did not believe that they were taken in Ireland. The most impressive view from the bridge in my opinion was of Carrick-a-Rede Island. The next landmark, the Giant's Causeway is only 25 minutes away from the bridge. This famous attraction is ideal for a walk and to relax, but is especially interesting for Star Trek fans as it is said to have inspired the set to one of their films.

While you're visiting Belfast and travelling on to Bushmills, if you're a fan of 'Game of Thrones', you'll find much to do and see in this part of Ireland. Much of the filming is done here. You'll most likely find that many people you meet have worked as an 'extra' in an episode or two. There are many 'Game of Thrones' tour operators, some offering more ex-

Ballycastle, County Antrim, Northern Ireland

tensive tours than others. So, if this is for you, I'd recommend doing a little research online first.

📍 *National Trust, 44 Causeway Road, Bushmills, County Antrim, UK BT57 8SU, +44 28 2073 1855,* ↗ nationaltrust.org.uk

From here on it's only a short trip along the coast until you reach the small town of Bushmills. It was named after the river 'Bush' and the watermills which were built there during the 1st century. Bushmills is 100 km away from Belfast and particularly known for one of the oldest distilleries on the whole island. **THE BUSHMILLS DISTILLERY** is situated idyllically on the north coast of Ireland and has a long history of whiskey production. The ongoing dispute with Locke's Distillery in Kilbeggan about which is actually the oldest distillery in Ireland is unfortunately not easily solved or settled. As a matter of fact, Bushmills received its license to produce whiskey in 1608, however, there are no documents which could prove that they were actually producing whiskey at this time. Since 1784 the distillery has been marked on maps, but it was initially nowhere near as successful as it is today. In 1802 James Mc Colgan and Patrick Corrigan brought the distillery to its new glory. After the death of Patrick Corrigan in 1865, his widow Ellen Jane (E.J.Corrigan) took over his part of the busi-

The Old Bushmills Distillery, Bushmills, County Antrim, Northern Ireland

ness. This was unusual at the time as women normally didn't take part in any businesses. Nevertheless, she became the managing director of the Company in 1890, while James Mc Colgan was responsible for manufacturing the whiskey. It was Ellen Jane who introduced electricity to the production lines in the factory, which was a small revolution for the end of the 19th century. The most important thing for Ellen Jane, as well as for George Roe, Powers and Jameson, was the quality of the products. She was one of those who supported the regulation that whiskey produced in a column still should be sold under a separate name. The advantage for Bushmills was that it owned four ships: S.S. Bushmills, S.S. City of Belfast, S.S. Dunmurry and S.S.Seamew. These were not only used to transport whiskey, but the ships gave Bushmills a competitive edge, an edge that Bushmills knew how to use. Thus Bushmills

– unlike Kilbeggan – managed to survive the hard times of war and the US prohibition almost unharmed and remain in business to this day. In 1972 Bushmills joined Irish Distillers. In 2005 the distillery was sold to DIAGEO and since 2014 it is owned by Don Julio. The Bushmills original is an 'Irish blended Whiskey', also referred to as 'White Bush' or 'Bushmills White Label'. It is a combination of malted barley and 'Single Grain Whiskey'. To begin with, the alcohol is stored in barrels made of American oak, but at the very end it is transferred to former sherry-barrels. This process gives the whiskey a soft and creamy consistency and a beautiful aroma of vanilla and fruits as well as a hint of chocolate.

📍 *Old Bushmills Distillery Co Ltd, 2 Distillery Road,*
Bushmills, Co.Antrim, UK, BT57 8XH
+44 2820733218 or +44 2820733272 ↗ **bushmills.com**

Those with not much time on their hands will be able to find a good road connection from here back to Belfast or Dublin. The lucky ones among you with more time can travel along the coast or directly to Derry, from where it's only a short way to an almost forgotten corner of Ireland – County Donegal.

The city of **DERRY/LONDONDERRY** is situated on the coast, directly at the border of both countries. The Northern Irish name is Londonderry and in the Republic of Ireland it is called Derry. Don't let yourself be confused, it really is the same city. For those with an interest in history, I would highly recommend a stop here. The most famous attractions are the Free Derry Corner, The Bloody Sunday Memorial, the People's Gallery Murals and the museum of Free Derry.

↗ discovernorthernireland.com
↗ visitderry.com

Apprentice Boy's Memorial Hall,
Derry or Londonderry, Northern Ireland

Here in the north of Ireland in County Derry, right beside the Peace Bridge and almost in Derry City centre is the **QUIET MAN CRAFT DISTILLERY**. This is located on, what was formerly Ebrington Navel base. There are plans to rejuvenate the original buildings as a fully functional distillery and also a visitor centre. Situated on the River Foyle, the plan for this complex is for a hotel, maritime museum and the distillery. In the old Admirals Building you'll find the three pot stills used for the whiskey and also a fourth pot still where they will produce gin. Ciaran Mulgrew, the managing director and one of the owners of the distillery will, in the small garden on the riverside, grow plants for the gin production. On the tour, you'll get an overview of the long whiskey history of the town, learn what is special about distilling whiskey and the difference between mak-

ing it and gin. You'll also learn a bit about the history of Derry City. Of course, don't forget the testing part. I personally cannot wait until the visitor centre opens its doors in 2020. The distillery is part of Niche Drinks Company, which is famous for producing crème liquors. This is probably why it's no surprise that they want to have their own

Admirals Building, Ebrington Navel base, County Derry

brand name. It will be called 'Quiet Man' and while that's also the name of a film made in Ireland in 1952, starring John Wayne and Maureen O'Hara, its name came about to honour the founder's father, who worked in a pub tending the bar and was known to be a quiet man.

📍 *The Derry Craft Distillery, Museum and Restaurant,*
11-17 Ebrington Barracks, Derry, Derry, BT47 6NS, N. Ireland
+44 2871343434, ↗ nichedrinks.com

Once you leave Derry, you are back on Irish ground. People without EU identification or passports should inform themselves in advance about entry requirements.

Dunlewey Lough, Glenveagh National Park, County Donegal

County Donegal consists mainly of mountains and is therefore ideal for people who love hiking. Furthermore, it mostly consists of small villages and towns so you will encounter a lot of nature, but not so many people. Here you can truly be alone, or on your own, if that's what you want. For almost a century, this county has had Northern Ireland sharing its land border, apart from a few kilometres in its south west extreme. It actually extends further north than what is known as Northern Ireland too. Confused? I was. It's mostly accessible by narrow roads and often referred to as 'The forgotten'. For example, there isn't even a train connection to this part of Ireland. The most northern point in Ireland, located in Donegal, is **MALIN HEAD**. The climate in Donegal is influenced by the Gulf Stream, which means mild and moist summers and mild, wet winters. Due to the fact that Donegal is so remote it has always been the perfect spot to secretly produce poitín, which led to its nickname 'Poitín Maker'. There's still a figure quoted that at times, there were up to 1,500 secret poitín distilleries in County Donegal.

Co. Donegal has a lot of Irish speakers and designated Gaeltacht areas. The most direct way from Derry to the next distillery is through the town of Donegal, however, if you have time to spare, I would recommend taking the N56. This road will lead you along the coast and through picturesque little villages until you have reached our next destination **CARRICK** in County Donegal. I truly am of the opinion that this is one of the most beautiful spots in Ireland. Here you can admire the cliffs of Donegal in a leisurely manner, without having to jostle amid large crowds for the best spot. The **SLIEVE LEAGUE CLIFFS** are the sixth highest sea cliffs in Europe and three times as high as the more famous Cliffs of Moher! It is definitely worth spending time here. ↗sliabhliag.com/visitor-centre

The second very good reason to stop in Carrick is the small, but excellent **SLIABHLIAG DISTILLERY**. You will find it in a place where time stands still. It's nestled into a post-card-like landscape, surrounded by mountains, yet also beside the sea and situated at the end of the world or at the start of Europe – depending on your point of view. The distillery currently resides in temporary quarters while awaiting the completion of the new distillery. It is planned to give more than an overview about the whiskey, gin and poitín production and of course, you will get the opportunity to taste these delicacies. Since 1841, the

Whiskey from Sliabhliag Distillery

SliabhLiag Distillery has been the only official distillery in this area. I am particularly looking forward to the poitín museum which will be built next to the distillery. There are many stories about the smuggling of the secretly produced alcohol from here to Scotland, which led to the situation of having more taxmen than police on the streets of Donegal.

📍 *Sliabhliag Distillery, Line Road, Carrick, F94 X9DX, Co. Donegal*
+353 749739875, ↗ sliabhliagdistillery.com

If you head south in the direction of Sligo on the N15, you will arrive at the town of **DONEGAL**. Especially worth seeing are **DONEGAL ABBEY** and the ruins of **DONEGAL CASTLE**. I can also recommend the boat tour.
Waterbus, +353 749 72 3666, ↗ donegalbaywaterbus.com

If you leave Donegal in the direction of Sligo, you will drive along the border between Northern Ireland and the Republic of Ireland. You can tell by the road signs which country you are in. When the maximum speed is indicated in m/h you are in Northern Ireland, if its indicated in km/h, you are in the Republic. On the way to Sligo there are two spots I'd recommend seeing. The first one is the **PORCELAIN FACTORY** in Belleek. Belleek is one of the places directly situated on the border and therefore belongs to both the Republic and Northern Ireland. I wonder if you might need a passport to cross the road after Brexit? The factory is 160 years old and even nowadays everything is handmade. It's a real treat to see such craftsmanship with your own eyes.

The second stop, **LISADELL HOUSE** is especially interesting from a historical point of view. It was the home of Constance Markievicz and

her lesser known siblings, Eva Gore-Booth and Josslyn Gore-Booth. Countess Markievicz was one of the leading personalities of the 1916 rebellion and the first woman to be voted into the free Irish Parliament called 'Dáil Éireann'. The house represents for me, the history of a very brave woman. She was an artist who

Ballinfull House Lisadell, Ballinful, Co. Sligo

supported the poorest of society with great engagement – as had her father, Sir Henry Gore-Booth during the Famine, half a century earlier.

In Lisadell House you will also get a good picture of the living conditions at the beginning of the 20th century in Ireland. This includes information about the 'potato famine', a famine caused by potato blight, which had a devastating impact on the population of Ireland. It was one of the triggers for the waves of Irish emigrants going overseas. I was also impressed by the perfect location of this house - on the one hand you can see the Atlantic Ocean and on the other, you get a view of **BENBULBEN**, a high mountain on the outskirts of Sligo. It doesn't surprise me at all that the poet W.B. Yeats loved this place and spent a lot of time here.

♀ *Ballinfull House Lisadell, Ballinful, F91 YN72, Co. Sligo*
+353 71 9163450, ⌐lissadellhouse.com

Not far away from here and also well worth a visit is **SLIGO TOWN**. The town is nestled between Sligo Bay by the Atlantic and the foot of Benbulben and the Killery Mountains. This place is a must for all keen photographers. The sunsets are truly unique here. The **Lough Gill Distillery** (Hazelwood Demesne Ltd) is located here, but it is still in the making. I heard that this distillery produces whiskey, but unfortunately has no visitor centre as yet. That might be the reason why it proved difficult to get information about it. I don't know what the situation will be when you read this, but thought it worth including. Perhaps it is open to visitors by now.

♥ *Hazelwood Demesne, Hazelwood Calry, Co.Sligo*

Those who head in the direction of County Mayo will discover two more distilleries there. County Mayo is situated on the west coast of Ireland and known for its wild beauty. Please be mindful of the sheep. You'll encounter them everywhere. While they don't have great road sense, they're more than happy to pose for a photo or two. Mayo is famous for its small islands and its steep cliffs. It is a heaven on earth for nature lovers. From hiking and climbing to fishing or hunting – everything is possible. Whiskey fans will not be disappointed either.

The first distillery that I would like to introduce to you can be reached after a 90-minute drive on the N59 from Sligo to Lahardane. There you will find the **Nephin Whiskey Company Ltd**, a family business with an ad-joining farm that supplies everything the distillery needs for its whiskey production. The visitor centre is still under construction, please check on their website to find out if you can visit the distillery when you travel here.

♥ *Nephin Whiskey Company Ltd, Lahardane, F26 W2H9 Co. Mayo* *+353 965 1717,* ➚nephinwhiskey.com

The second distillery in County Mayo is located at the other side of **Lough Conn**, in the northern part of the county. It doesn't matter whether you drive from the north or the south, from the Nephin Whiskey Company you will need 30 minutes either way. The **Connacht Whiskey Company** is housed in the former family bakery. You could say the family remained loyal to the grain production – merely changing bread for whiskey. The

three copper stills differ from the Irish standard. They do, however, guarantee a unique taste. The barrels containing the raw alcohol are brought by the owner to a small island in the hope that the whiskey will be refined by the sea air. Like many other modern and new distilleries, Connacht not only produces whiskey, but also vodka and poitín, which it calls 'Strawboys', named after an old wedding tradition. In former

Pot Stills, Connacht Whiskey Company, Belleek, Co. Mayo

times the Strawboys visited weddings, where they would dance with the bride and other women. They would play music, sing and entertain with jokes and good humour. The men dressed in straw costumes and wore straw hats to cover their faces. The ritual was meant to bring luck, health and prosperity. The founders of this distillery, three Americans and one Irish person carried out their dream to bring a distillery to the West of Ireland again.

 ♀ The Connacht Whiskey Co. Ltd, Castle Road
 Belleek, Ballina, F26 P932, Co. Mayo
 +353 967 4598, ↗ connachtwhiskey.com

Now you could go further in the direction of Castlebar, Westport and Galway, or stick with us and get to know two more distilleries. You can either travel back on the N59 towards Sligo and change onto the R284, or you can start on the R294 which will later merge into the R284. In Ireland, you'll always be offered a choice when asking for directions. I was once told, 'Now, If I were you, I wouldn't start from here.' In any case you should plan enough time for this trip. The word 'fast' does not actually exist in Ireland.

THE SHED DISTILLERY OF P.J. has, like many others, not only whiskey on offer, but also gin and 'Potato Vodka'. As the name indicates the distillery is decorated and designed like a shed. Visitors can wander through the 'shed' and observe the processes of the whiskey production. The reconstruction works were finished in the summer of 2017 and everything is now reopened and accessible. The three pot stills – one of them originated in Germany as did one of the investors – come in a special shape. Due to the connection with Germany, the gin produced in this distillery can be bought in many German shops. Currently it is not possible to buy their whiskey as it hasn't been stored long enough, so for the time being we can only indulge in gin and vodka.

📍 *The Shed Distillery of P.J., Rigney Carrick Road, Drumshanbo, N41 R6D7, Co. Leitrim, +353 86 396 5740*
↗ **thesheddistillery.com**

Gin Pot Still, Shed Distillery

Approximately an hour from Drumshanbo, via the N4 and L1405 (please be careful as the roads are quite narrow and not always very well maintained), you will reach Lanesborough. A worthwhile detour, whether just to stretch your legs in beautiful surroundings or to have a refreshment in the coffee shop of the magnificent Strokestown Park, House, Gardens and National Famine Museum. Those with time on their hands and an interest in Irish history, will find a lot there, but you will need three or four hours – or even a whole day for this.

At the top of the Lake **LOUGH REE**, there is building work going on for a new family business and distillery, **LOUGH REE DISTILLERY**. The family, who are from this area, envision combining the old traditions with modern techniques to create a perspective for the future – not only for themselves, but also for the region. As with many stories around the topic of whiskey, where myths and tales merge to a poetic whole, the history of the distilling building also has a spiritual element. The family accidentally discovered an historical Georgian building, close to a 1,000-year-old bridge by the River Shannon. They knew immediately that they had found the perfect place to put their plans into action. There is enough space for the production site and equipment, warehouses and a visitor centre. The plan is to primarily produce whiskey (Premium Single Cask Whiskey, Single Pot Still, Single Malt), but also other spirits like gin, vodka, poitín, liquor and fruit schnapps. As stated, the distillery is still under construction, but is due to open in 2019.

♥ *Lough Ree Distillery, Main St., Lanesborough, Co. Longford*
+353 43 335 1250 **↗** **lrd.ie**
♥ *Strokestown Park, House, Gardens and National Famine Museum*
+353 71 9633013 **↗** **strokestownpark.ie**

Lough Ree

Lough Ree is one of three large lakes on the River Shannon. Geographically speaking they are in the middle of the island of Ireland. On **↗** **irishlakes.ie** you can find more information about activities in this area, for example, boat rental or fishing trips.

From here, you can head in the direction of Athlone and from there, on to the motorway back to Dublin, however, if you still haven't had enough whiskey and haven't visited there already, it's easy to continue towards **TULLAMORE** and **KILBEGGAN**. You will find out more about these in the Chapter 'East-West Tour'.

"*The true pioneer of civilization is not the newspaper, not religion, not the railroad but whiskey!*"
Mark Twain

Discover the South

As the saying for some here goes: 'All roads lead to Cork'. This expression could not be truer, as there are many activities available in the south of the island.I have listed some options below.

1. If you want to get there directly, take the M7/M8 motorways. Along this stretch of motorway, you will find an apple brandy distillery (p.s. maybe save this for when you don't plan to drive) and Irish Distillers in Midleton. Irish Distillers include household names like that of Jameson, Powers, Redbreast and Green Spot.

2. On the way down south, in the counties of Carlow and Waterford along the M9 motorway, there are five whiskey distilleries that are open to the public. Further on in Co. Cork lies Midleton, which not only offers whiskey, but also a beer brewery and its own house specialities: schnapps, liqueur and organic apple products.

3. Following the east coast of the island you can be sure to find every sort of brewery and distillery, making the journey a really interesting one.

4. The trip gets even more interesting if you follow the enchanting landscapes of the Wild Atlantic Way which passes through Limerick and all the way to Dingle. This stretch continues further south into West Cork and Kerry where you can find another three distilleries and a separate whiskey trader.

If you want to be particularly adventurous and get the most out of your travels, you can always connect the different routes together to make your own personalised trip. If you feel the urge to visit all the distilleries and locations, then hurray for you. I think we'd get along very well! All in all, just remember to enjoy yourself and take in the beauty of the island and have 'a wee bit of craic!'

TOUR 1 – THROUGH CORK AND MIDLETON USING THE M7/M8

When driving from Dublin take the M50 aka the Dublin Ring Road that connects to the M7. This goes through Newbridge (home of the National Horse Stud), Kildare, and Portlaoise on the M8.

Kildare Town

When on the M8 you have some options for short breaks. The **TIPPERARY BOUTIQUE DISTILLERY** is located on the grange of a local family. In the 17th and 18th centuries, the farmers were clever and used the available proximity of fresh water to plant barley and some of the remainder of their land to store whiskey barrels. This is how the owners of this Tipperary Farm and many others came to the idea of taking the step to broaden their whiskey business. Unfortunately, neither the farm nor the distillery is open for visitation at the moment, but when it is, it definitely will be a worthy stop on your whiskey travels!

📍 *Tipperary Boutique Distillery Ltd., Newtownadam, Cahir, Co. Tipperary* ↗ tipperarydistillery.ie

Lovers of old churches and castles should take a look at the towns of Cashel and Cahir that are directly off the M8 motorway. If you are in and around Cashel, one of the interesting sites is the former cloisters and church fortress that is the **'ROCK OF CASHEL'**. The name 'rock' comes from the fact the structure was built on a sixty metre high rock which overlooks the wide expansive meadows and fields of Co. Tipperary. In the middle of the town Cahir, there is also Cahir Castle. Both towns are steeped in history and can be traced back to the 12th and 13th centuries. If you look carefully, you'll see a cannonball lodged in the wall of Cahir Castle.

♀ *Cahir Castle, Castle St., Townparks, Cahir, Co. Tipperary*
+353 52 744 1011, ↗ **heritageireland.ie**
Rock of Cashel, Moor, Cashel, Co. Tipperary,
+353 62 61437, ↗ **cashel.ie**

Cahir Castle, Cahir, Co. Tipperary

To throw some more fun options out there, the Mitchelstown Caves, which are part of an extensive cave system in Ireland, can be a nice out-doorsy detour on your way down south. On the tours through the Mitchels-town cave tunnels, you can explore the generous works of art nature has put on display, i.e. stalagmites, stalactites and huge calcite towers. One of the prettiest natural formations in Europe is that of the nine-metre-high 'Tower of Babel'.

♀ *Mitchelstown Cave, Burncourt, Cahir, Co. Tipperary*
+353 52 746 7246

The **Longueville House Cider and Apple Distillery** is a family owned business where you can find a hotel, restaurant, and a small brewery.

We chanced upon this gem while at the 'Whiskey Live' event in Dublin. The most memorable drink from this event was the whiskey that came from this little known place. Shem and I were so impressed we kept wondering for the rest of the event, where this light and tasty surprise came from. We kept going around in circles if it was pot still made and Irish, or did it possibly wander all the way here from a French distillery? Maybe, when you have a taste, you'll come up with your own wild assumptions.

Longueville House, Mallow

📍 *Longueville House*
Mallow, P51 KC8K,
Co. Cork, +353 22 47459
↗ longuevillehouse.ie

Cork is the second largest city in Ireland. This beautiful second city is sometimes called the real capital by Corkonians, or even 'The People's Republic of Cork'. The city itself holds significant geographical importance due to its proximity to the sea and it also sits on the River Lee. The city centre is a bit quirkier than some would find Dublin, but that is part of its charm! That being said, there are lots of small shops with all the touristy stuff a visitor could want. In a new city, I always get a bit confused by the layout and to avoid any embarrassing car stalls or overall misery on my part, I prefer to just park the car and use public transport, becoming a local so to say. Due to the sheer size of County Cork, I'm going to list a couple of detours, so that you can find your way through the city and many outer areas. As always do what feels best and visit the places that really hold your interest and I'm sure there will be plenty for you here in the 'Rebel County'!

Cork City

Unfortunately during the wars between England and Ireland, most of the historical landmarks and many old buildings were completely destroyed. Not to worry, Cork City and close surroundings still has old time charm to be found around every corner.

Here are some exploring options: **THE BUTTER MUSEUM**, **THE ENGLISH MARKET**, **BLACKROCK CASTLE OBSERVATORY**, **BLARNEY CASTLE**, **CHARLES FORT**.

ST. ANNE'S CATHEDRAL with the Shandon Bells is also close to the Butter Museum and its weather vane is a golden fish. You can see it on the skyline from some parts of the city and you might even get to climb its tower and

Cork City (top), Cobh

ring its famous bells. There's a big clock on each face of the tower, although I wouldn't set my watch by it. Due to it frequently showing incorrect times on each clock, it's affectionately known as 'the four-faced liar.'

Another worthy visit is to Cobh which is about 30 minutes outside the city on the R624. In this cosy little coastal town there is a museum-like exhibition that documents emigration from Ireland during the times of the Potato Famine and other periods of hardship. For any fans of the Titanic, Cobh is a must as this was the last place the ship dropped anchor before it sailed on through the Atlantic. In the **COBH HERITAGE CENTRE** (Cobh the Titanic Experience, ↗visitcobh.com) visitors will definitely get their money's worth. There is also a regular commuter train serving it from Cork and while not quite the Orient Express, I have a friend who used this service daily for years and says he never tired of it.

One of the nicest Breweries in Cork is the **ST. PATRICK'S DISTILLERY LIMITED**. Unfortunately, it doesn't have a visitor centre, or even any plan as of now to build one. The lack of visitor centre is more than made up for by the amount of effort that goes into the quality of spirits produced here, i.e. whiskey, gin and vodka varieties. A little specialty of this brewery is the fact that they use potatoes in their production of gin and vodka and this gives the drinks a soft sweet flavour. For those of you who are conscious of gluten, these gin and vodka drinks are free of the pesky protein.

♥ *St. Patrick's Distillery Ltd., Unit 105, St. Patrick's Mills, Douglas, T12 YE0C, Co. Cork,* ↗ stpatricksdistillery.ie

About 30 minutes away, or 25 km (via N25) from Cork City, is the town of **MIDLETON**. Midleton was founded in the 11th century by the Normans and later populated by Cistercian monks. The town lies near the Owenacurra River and its name is simple enough in its origins as it lies between Cork City and Youghal, so pretty much 'middle town'. Youghal in its heyday was an important centre for trade and garrisoning of soldiers.

Midleton, given its central location, was known for being a post or mail depot and later on, in 1670, it was renamed 'Post City' of the 'Great Southern and Western Railway'. Like many other towns at this time and

Pot still and watermill from the Old Midleton Distillery, Midleton, Co. Cork

during the 19th century in general, Irish whiskey production here suffered. Ireland at this time was going through the 'Great Hunger' where many towns and families suffered from what originally came from a shortage of potatoes, caused by a blight for two years in succession. Due to the dramatic impact of this famine, the domestic demand for whiskey plummeted and many breweries had to close their doors. As a countermeasure in 1860, the owner of Midleton distillery James Murphy suggested that other local distilleries band together to reduce costs. This suggestion led to the merger of the **DALY'S DISTILLERY**, **THE GREEN**, **NORTH MALL** and **THE WATERCOURSE**. In 1868, the **JAMES MIDLETON DISTILLERY** joined the local association and this arrangement continued until 1966.

Whiskey collection from Irish Distillers Limited, Midleton, Co. Cork

Adding to the hardships, in 1920, a devastating fire destroyed the five mills that made up the North Mall Distillery. Since the Irish whiskey industry was in a period of crisis and there was no financial backing to support the rebuild of the mills, this meant that a piece of Irish history went up in flames, literally, and was lost forever. Due to the unstable economy it was decided that all of the production efforts would be focused in Midleton. Thus Midleton, for the second time in its history, became the saviour of Irish whiskey. Since times were still unstable for the whiskey business, the **CORK DISTILLERY COMPANY** ultimately amalgamated with the remaining Dublin distilleries of John Jameson and Son and John Powers & Son, to create Irish Distillers.

Irish Distillers Limited originated in 1966 from the Cork Distillery Company, **JOHN JAMESON & SON** and also **JOHN POWERS & SON**. The goal of this coming together was, in principle, to save the art and business of Irish whiskey. The distilleries in Dublin were shut down in order to accommodate the relocation of all the manpower to Midleton in Co. Cork. This created the basis for the distilleries to unite together and therefore produce a positive change for the industry. The banding together of the distilleries had a domino effect on other distillers and **BUSHMILLS** also joined Irish Distillers in 1972.

In 1975, a new complex was built in Midleton and the buildings of the **OLD MIDLETON DISTILLERY** and the **JAMESON'S BOW STREET DISTILLERY** were transformed into visitor centres. In 2016, the Old Midleton Distillery expanded and opened up a pot still facility, for training and test purposes. As for the Jameson's Bow Street Distillery, they revamped the business and since March 2017, is once again an active distillery.

Famous brands that come from the Irish Distillers Group are **JAMESON WHISKEY**, **POWERS WHISKEY**, **MIDLETON WHISKEY**, and also **PADDY WHISKEY** (while now owned by Sazerac, they have contracted their production to Midleton). **REDBREAST WHISKEY** and also **GREEN SPOT**, which was previously exclusive to bonders, are now also produced here with the maturing process unchanged. Redbreast were part of the Gilbey brand and Green Spot was owned by Mitchell & Son Wine Merchants, but are now both owned by **IRISH DISTILLERS LTD.**

📍 *Irish Distillers Ltd, Distillery Walk, Midleton, Co. Cork,*
+353 1 807 2348, ↗ jamesonwhiskey.com/tours

TOUR 2 – THROUGH CARLOW AND WATERFORD (VIA M9)

If you want to experience some of the different flavours of Ireland, I would suggest, after you've seen the sights and tasted something of what the old town of Kilkenny has to offer, that you head on to Waterford on the N10 and M9. Another possibility is to take the N80 and go through the small town of Clonegal. Taking the N80 is ideal for those who want to see the ever-changing landscapes of Ireland's countryside. The town of Clone-

Huntington Castle, Clonegal, Co. Carlow

gal rests between the borders of Counties Wexford, Carlow, and Wicklow. Located on the Derry River, the town is only a few kilometres away from where the Derry and Slaney Rivers join together. In earlier times the town was an important military post and was later built into a castle.

HUNTINGTON CASTLE is still inhabited by its ancestral family, but is open to the public for visits. Along with the charms of the castle, you can also find the ruins of the **'SIMON LACY DISTILLERY'**, which was in use from 1798 to 1806.

After a fire, the distillery was not rebuilt. The mother of the farmer and owner of this land, can still recall how it provided good opportunities for

Simon Lacy Distillery (1798 to 1806), Clonegal, Co. Wexford

work in the area. In the glory days of whiskey, there were around eleven malt houses in the area. If you find yourself wandering through the town and taking in the scenery, you could do worse than drop in to **OSBORNE'S BAR & LOUNGE**. This is one of the oldest pubs in Ireland and you'll see, on entering, that this place has a lot of history built into it.

Further on from Clonegal, you can drive in the direction of Carlow on the N80. After about 30 minutes on the N80, if you turn off at the exit 'Ballon' through the R 724 you will arrive in a place called Bagenalstown. There you'll find the **WALSH WHISKEY DISTILLERY** and from here you can continue the tour at your own pace.

The **KILKENNY TOUR** is included in the Dublin section 'The Outskirts of Dublin'. This tour includes the Walsh Whiskey Distillery, the **HIGHBANK ORGANIC FARM**, **KILBALLYKEEFE DISTILLERY**, **SMITHWICK'S KILKENNY** and the town of Kilkenny with the **KILKENNY WHISKEY GUILD**.

In case that you don't want to risk being pulled over and made to take a breathalyser from all these distillery tours, you can easily take a taxi from Highbank Organic Farm to Kilballykeefe Distillery as they are only about ten minutes away from each other. The Highbank Organic Farm has been modernised and offers bookings for a double-room stay through Airbnb ... so look at it as a chance to get cozy as it only houses four people.

From Kilkenny onwards, you will have to get on the M9 to travel to **WATERFORD**. Waterford is a harbour city on the south east coast of the island. It was founded in 914 BC by the Vikings. This makes it one of the oldest cities in Ireland. Parts of the city, like that of the old city walls and

Waterford Town, Co. Waterford

the Reginald Tower are still intact, while other archaeological finds are on display at the **MUSEUM OF TREASURES**.

The **WATERFORD DISTILLERY** was built on a site that formerly housed another distillery, founded in 1792 by William Strangman. On the grounds of the old brewery, you can still see some of the original machinery used at the time of its inception. Since 2013, the old buildings and machines of the Waterford Distillery have been used by Guinness. In 2014, Mark Reynier acquired the brewery and it now functions again as a distillery. Mark Reynier began his career in the spirits industry by starting out marketing wine. Mark knew that depending on the area the wine was produced in, there was a marked difference in the quality and taste of the wine. He decided to take his interest and knowledge and use it to his advantage in the whiskey business. The first important step was to avoid mixing the

Waterford Distillery, Waterford, Co. Waterford,

different varieties of barley that were being purchased, instead, keeping them in groups. Every delivery from then on was prepared separately, distilled and stored. With every bottle of whiskey from Waterford Distillery, there is a code on the back that will tell you where the barley came from, where and when it was produced and also how long it was stored for. With this distillery, there is total transparency.

After some time and a lot of curiosity, we found the suppliers and some of the farmers of this organic barley. Unfortunately, we'll need a little bit of patience before we can try the finished product. Currently the brewery is only available for visits by appointment, but Mark Reynier is contemplating making this gem even more sparkling by adding a visitor centre.

♥ *Waterford Distillery, 9 Mary Street, Waterford, Co. Waterford,*
+353 51 303 508, ↗ waterforddistillery.ie

The **HOUSE OF WATERFORD CRYSTAL** is a well known factory both here and abroad and has been going strong since its founding in 1793. Just a wee tip, if you are looking for some beautiful whiskey glasses to accompany all those nice 'souvenirs' that you pick up, this is the place to find them. Visitors are welcome.

♥ *House of Waterford Crystal, +353 51 317 000*
↗ waterfordvisitorcentre.com

At this point you can decide how you will go on from here. If you keep going on the N25, you can continue on to Midleton and Cork, more of which you can find in the earlier section 'Through Cork and Midleton.

Our next distillery can be found in a town called **KILMACTHOMAS**, around 30 minutes from Waterford on the N25. Maybe by this point you'll feel you have sat too long in the car … if that's the case then this place will ideally suit your needs. Here in Kilmacthomas you will find yourself surrounded by nature, giving a nice break from the continuous drag of being on the road. The former railway lines have been turned into nature paths for cyclists and walkers and go in the direction of **DUNGARVAN**. The good thing about this little outing is that you can also rent a bike to stretch your legs at either end of the track.

The **GORTINORE DISTILLERY** is a quirky place, built in an old mill. There are plans for three pot stills to be built, so that the whiskey can be brewed in the traditional fashion. By Autumn 2019, the building should

Old mill and the future Gortinore Distillery , Kilmacthomas, Co. Waterford

be finished which means the distilling and brewing can begin (lucky us!). In the coffee shop, they offer alcoholic and non-alcoholic drinks. For me, an Irish coffee and apple tart will always do the trick.

📍 *Gortinore Distillery, Kilmacthomas, Co. Waterford,*
+353 86 794 3033, ↗ gortinore.com

Another worthwile visit in Kilmacthomas is a housing estate called the **WORKHOUSE**. It was built between 1848 and 1850. This is one of many places in Ireland that housed people in poverty during the potato famine and later, due to work shortages, those who could not pay their rent. The British built around fifty of these social houses. On the grounds of the workhouse there is a church that has separate areas for men, women and children, because at that time, families could not have contact with each other while living there. The goal of this separation tactic was actually to discourage people from living there longer than was necessary. Many landlords added to this by buying and offering families tickets oversees, to speed up the process of emptying the living quarters. Unfortunately, lots of these families never survived the journeys across the seas to destinations like Australia, Canada and the USA.

Since this part of history has always been a stain on Irish history, the Workhouse in Kilmacthomas is even more important today as a symbol of hope, that history will not repeat itself. The area of Kilmacthomas is currently going through a rebuilding and restoration phase to try and shake off some of its gloomier past. If you have an interest in this topic, you can find more information at the Irish Workhouse Centre in Portumna Co. Galway. If you are in the area between the borders of Co. Galway and Co. Clare, it would be worth taking a detour to the visitor centre and getting a broader insight into the history of this era.

Clock Gate, Youghal, Co. Cork

An hour away from Kilmacthomas (off the N25) you will find the small town of **YOUGHAL**. In the 11th century, the Vikings came here and created a settlement. Youghal is the perfect place to have a relaxed vacation thanks to its fine sandy beaches and the many day trips you can take to nearby places. Also, for anyone that loves to go outdoor exploring there are plenty of places to wander about while taking in the fresh air. A particularly interesting feature of the town is the **CLOCK GATE** which was built in 1777, along with the castle and city walls that unfortunately, are now quite run down. From 1837, the Clock Gate was used as a prison and then later on, in 1959, it was transformed into a housing area where many families now live.

In Youghal, you can find several houses (alms houses and the Town Hall) that were built in the 17th century. After its heyday, Youghal became more and more a thing of the past. Its previously important harbour, also became less useful for shipping as it wasn't deep enough to accommodate larger ships. Today, Youghal is a popular summer destination for many Cork families and it's also well known for the role it played in the filming of the 1950s movie **MOBY DICK**. Further on from the **MOBY DICK PUB**, you'll see a small stone house where you will find plenty of tourism information and can also purchase tickets for the Clock Gate. Right behind the tourist centre, you can find the Quay's Pub, where they have an extensive selection of whiskey, which may be just what you need after your day's activities.

↗ youghalchamber.ie

↗ youghal4all.com

Moby Dick Pub, the Quay's Pub, Youghal, Co. Cork

TOUR 3 – FROM DUBLIN TO WATERFORD (via N81, N80, N11 and N25 through Ballon, then along the east coast on the N11 to Enniscorthy, New Ross, Wexford)

The following tour begins on the N81, takes the direction Waterford/Clonegal and will continue on to Ballon where the motorway passes through the N80. You can keep going on this stretch of road till you reach Enniscorthy and from there, the fastest way is to take the N30 to New Ross and then onwards to Waterford. A nice little detour is to go through **ENNISCORTHY** on the N11 and follow that towards Wexford and then get off at the Hook Peninsula, so that you can continue on towards Waterford.

If you're not under any time constraints, a nice excursion while driving south from Dublin is a stop in Wicklow Town. You'll see it signposted as you travel along the M11/N11. Traveling down through the south east of the island through places like Enniscorthy and Waterford will give you the chance to see some places that are truly steeped in history, like the small town of Ferns. There you can find historical gems like the remains of old cloisters,

built in the 6th century. Ferns is of historical importance as it was the former capital of the Kingdom of Leinster. From this period, only the remains of the old castle are still preserved within the town. Enniscorthy also has historical significance. We can follow the history of the town all the way back to 465. The town's castle was built in 1205. Enniscorthy was one of the main locations for the film and book 'Brooklyn' by Colm Tóibín, who hails from the town. You can discover more history about the town and its surroundings in this book.

Enniscorthy Castle, Castle Hill, Enniscorthy, Co. Wexford

 ♥ *Enniscorthy Castle, Castle Hill, Enniscorthy, Co. Wexford,*
  +353 53 923 4699, ↗ **enniscorthytourism.com**

If you take the N11 from Enniscorthy, you can take a detour towards Wexford and then further on, with the N25 from New Ross to Waterford. If you don't have time to drive the picturesque Ring of Hook , you might head for New Ross where there is also plenty to see, particularly if you'd like to learn more about the Great Famine. The **Dunbrody Emigrant Ship** in **New Ross** (from Enniscourthy on to the N30) is a fine restoration of a sailboat that was rebuilt using its original parts. In the 1840s, ships were

a must for a country struggling through famine. This was a time when many Irish people who had little choice were forced to leave Ireland. A risky sea voyage was the lesser of two evils, compared to the low odds of survival during the famine. The restoration of the ship marks the commemoration and remembrance of an important time for the town.

Dunbrody Famine Ship Experience

 ♥ *Dunbrody Famine Ship Experience, The Quay, New Ross Co. Wexford, +353 51 425 239*

JOHNSTOWN CASTLE was the seat of two prominent families from **WEXFORD**. It was built in the 12th century by the Norman Esmonde family. In 1692, with the passing of various historical events, it came into the possession of John Grogan. The Castle lies on the border of Wexford and is under the protection of the 'Irish Heritage Trust'. In 2015, restoration work began in order to return the castle to its former glory.

📍 *Johnstown Castle Gardens Wexford*, **+353 53 918 4671**
↗ **johnstowncastlegardens.ie**   *Johnstown Castle Gardens, Wexford*

THE 'RING OF HOOK' COASTAL DRIVE

If time allows, you should without a doubt include this excursion in your itinary. Simply follow the N25 from Wexford along the coast, driving along narrow country roads. To help prepare yourself, you can easily find some more info on the website for **HOOK PENINSULA** where it will suggest some great sites to visit. This part of the island is in my opinion, very interesting, as here you will see both dramatic landscapes as well as historical events coming together. There are two things I want to single out: first is the **HOOK LIGHTHOUSE** which makes a great photo (by the way, the Hook Peninsula gives the expression 'by Hook or by Crook' to the English language). The second is **LOFTUS HALL**, built in 1350 and rumoured to have ghosts and spirits residing there. Some other worthy stops are: **TINTERN ABBEY** (built ca. 1200) & Colclough Walled Garden, Fethard Castle, Dollar Bay, Duncannon Village & Fort, Templetown Church Ruins, Limekiln, Churchtown Church, Saltmills Village, Baginbun Head & Martello Tower, Hook Windmill.

📍 *Hook Peninsula*, **+353 51 38 9530**
↗ **hookpeninsula.com**   *Hook Lighthouse, Co. Wexford*

When leaving the Hook Peninsula, take the N25 towards Waterford. From here on, follow the directions from the earlier Tour 2 section 'from Waterford through Kilmacthomas and Youghal' until you reach Midleton, home of Irish Distillers (see earlier chapter.)

TOUR 4 – FROM DUBLIN THROUGH LIMERICK AND DINGLE TO KERRY AND WEST CORK

Travelling from Dublin to Kerry, you'll get to drive through Limerick. To do this, take the N7 which will become the M7 at Naas and is a fairly quick way to reach the west side of the island.

On the way, you can stop in Co. Kildare and in **KILDARE TOWN**. Though it is the county capital, it's a small town built largely in the 5th century. Back then **SAINT BRIGID** founded the 'Church of

Cathedral Church of St. Brigid, Kildare Town

Oak' ('Cill Dara' in Irish which gave the name to Kildare) which unfortunately is no longer preserved. To make up for this historical loss there is now the Cathedral Church of St. Brigid.

Co. Kildare like many Irish places has a history with whiskey. A significant place here is the **CASSIDY'S DISTILLERY** in **MONASTEREVAN**, which was named Cassidy & Co. Monasterevan between the years of 1784 and 1921. In

Cassidy's Distillery, Monasterevan, Co. Kildare

1886, Alfred Barnard visited the distillery and stated that this small place was experienced in producing pure pot still whiskey. The whiskey was exclusively for local distribution. A memorable feature of this brewery was the mash and malt house that was built in the shape of a beehive. Sadly, this building was completely destroyed during restoration and nowadays, we only have the word of Mr. Barnard to go on. Of the rest of the 10-acre distillery, there's not much left of the former houses, but there are some older buildings that remain in good shape. There is a hope to rebuild the distillery and I have heard that one of its supporters and potential backers is none other than Bono of the Irish rock band U2. I will watch this space with interest.

Today this area of Ireland is well known for its horse breeding. Not far from Kildare you will find the **IRISH NATIONAL STUD & GARDENS**, which I'm sure will certainly interest any horse lovers reading this. An amusing event happens around March when all the new foals are born and the public can come and watch their capers and jump training.

Irish National Stud & Gardens, Tully

📍 *Irish National Stud & Gardens, Tully Kildare, Co. Kildare, R51 KX25, +353 45 521 617,* ↗ irishnationalstud.ie

R. & J. Wallace Distillery, Birr, Co. Offaly

If you have some time to spare, I would suggest visiting the small town of **BIRR** in Co. Offaly (the M7 and Roscrea exit, then switch to the N62). The town was built in the Georgian style. One of the recommended places to visit is **BIRR CASTLE** and gardens. It was built in 1170 and a peculiar feature is its astronomical telescope. It was built on a large mirror (1.83 meters) in 1845. For decades this telescope has been a unique sensation for Co. Offaly and to this day is still used for special projects.

📍 *Birr Castle, Rosse Row, Birr, R42 PD79, Co. Offaly +353 57 912 0336,* ↗ birrcastle.com

The town of Birr can also look back on its 100 years of whiskey traditions. It's well known that in 1805, four small breweries existed, though in 1807 three of them closed. The last one was taken over in 1890 by the Wallace brothers. The knowledge that we have today about these breweries, like so many others, comes from the notes and information gathered by journalist Alfred Barnard. By strolling through the town, you can find the old Georgian buildings that have been newly restored, but which still hold their charm. The houses, while being old, have been substantially modernised, some repurposed. For example, one of the old town houses is now a B&B, another was turned into an apartment block and one is now being turned into a new distillery. For more information visit the website: ↗offalyhistory.com

Back to the M7 to continue in the direction of Limerick. You could also travel from Birr to Nenagh via bog roads, which doesn't make for the smoothest of driving, but offers good views of Ireland's bogland. From Nenagh, you can rejoin the M7 for a fairly short drive on to Limerick.

Walker's Distillery – close to Limerick Castle

LIMERICK is among the tenth largest cities in Ireland and is geographically located on the Shannon River. This privileged piece of land meant that before, and during the time of the Vikings, this was a place of community and trade. From the 12th century, Limerick has monuments like **KING JOHN'S CASTLE** on the Shannon River and **ST. MARY'S CATHEDRAL** that are open to tourists. During the 17th and 18th centuries, Limerick's harbour developed into one of the most notorious hubs for all varieties of trade. From what we know of some of the history from mainland Europe, many Jewish families settled near these strategic trading areas. The fact that there was a Jewish community in Limerick goes to show how important a harbour like this was at the time. In correspondence to this growth in diversity and trade, **WALKER'S DISTILLERY** was also founded around this time, opening in 1820 and distilling for one year short of a century.

This was not the only distillery to be established then, but it was certainly one of the more prestigious ones visited by Alfred Barnard and later, described in his book. The brewery sits on the River Shannon and offers a beautiful view of the neighbouring farm houses and Limerick city. The brewery was one of the more modern buildings at the time. This brewery had the customary three copper stills and many employees, who lived on the distillery grounds. The distillery produced whiskey, described as pot still Irish whiskey by Barnard, that was sold throughout Ireland and was also exported to Great Britain. Like many of the Irish distilleries, Walkers Distillery did not survive the whiskey crisis. There are still pubs in Limerick where you can find advertisements and old pictures of Walker's Distillery. One of these pubs is **MICHAEL FLANNERY'S** on Denmark

Michael Flannery's Pub, Limerick city, Co. Limerick

Street. Today, the only remains of the former brewery are that of the old Georgian style Manor House, now known as the **'WALNUT HOUSE'.**

A few words about Michael Flannery's pub. In our quest for old whiskey and relics from former breweries, as well as tasting different whiskeys, my friend and driver Shem and I did not get the same welcome everywhere we visited. Obviously we couldn't try every single whiskey that was on offer there, but what we can say is that from what we tried, this pub has got it right. They make their own blend of whiskey which Michael Flannery's grandfather introduced long ago. It was also pleasant to get a welcome from many of the customers who'd come in for a quiet pint and perhaps a 'ball of malt' too.

📍 *Michael Flannery's Pub, 17 Denmark St., Limerick City, V94 T9W3, Co. Limerick, +353 61 436 677,* ↗ *flannerysbar.ie*

From here, your tour could go one of two ways. If you go in the direction of Cork and continue on, possibly because you are already familiar with Kerry and West Cork or maybe because you don't have much time,

then take the N20 to Cork. The N20 winds through typical Irish green landscapes where in the distance you can see mountains rising and from time to time a few Celtic crosses and some old city walls. An example of this is **BLARNEY CASTLE**, which is only a stone's throw away from Cork city. It's here you'll also find the famous Blarney Stone, although for reasons I won't go into here, I wouldn't recommend kissing it.

Blarney Castle

If you're in the mood for some further exploring and still have time, hop on the N69 towards Tralee and further on to Dingle. This is the fastest way of getting from place to place, plus it offers the chance to see a bit more of Ireland's more rugged and wild countryside. On this particular route there are two detours you can take.

The first is the small town of **ASKEATON**, which was founded directly on the shores of the Deel River. The historical structures of the Franciscan cloisters were built in 1389, but the real jewel of the town is **DESMOND CASTLE**, built in 1199.

Askeaton Castle, Co. Limerick

The second worthwhile stop is in **LISTOWEL** on the Feale River. This town is frequently described as the 'Literary Capital of Ireland', due to the fact that famous authors, like that of Bryan MacMahon and John B. Keane have lived here. Listowel is also home to the annual Listowel Writers' Week. It is situated right in the heart of Co. Kerry and is well known for its dairy farms and at the time of writing, had just received the overall award for being Ireland's tidiest town. Due to its well-preserved architectural heritage and its historical presence, Listowel became and remains, a notable town of Ireland. One of the architectural sights I would recommend is **LISTOWEL CASTLE**, built in 1303.

While you're here, why not pay a visit to John B's Bar where his son Billy, a fine poet himself, still pulls pints. If you hit it at the right time, Mickey Mulcreevy might be singing some of his well known, and not so well known hilarious songs.

TRALEE lies on a far outpost, almost like the 'rib' of the Dingle Peninsula, on the shores of the River Lee. Until the 8th century, Tralee was the biggest town in Ireland, but today it's best known for its 'Rose of Tralee International Festival', where a young lady is voted to become the 'Rose of Tralee'. In this function and for a whole year, she represents the town of Tralee, Kerry and the Republic of Ireland. Many of the women, although having Irish heritage are here for the first time. It's an important event for the Irish diaspora worldwide, as it allows young women with Irish roots to get in touch with their heritage and culture for a whole year.

Tralee lies in an old valley that is south of the Slieve Mountain range. In this valley there is an old boulder called Scotia's gravestone, where allegedly, the daughter of an Egyptian Pharaoh was laid to rest

Tower Mill in Blennville (top), Rose of Tralee, Tralee

The Anglo-Normans founded Tralee in the 13th century and built a castle to show its strategic importance. A fire would later almost completely destroy the city during the Desmond Rebellion, where the people resisted the rule of Queen Elizabeth I. The modern look of Tralee today comes largely from the 19th century, when the town was prospering and experiencing a lot of renovation. You can catch a glimpse of how the town used to look from the Georgian styled streets of 1826, which are part of what would have been the Castle grounds.

The **DINGLE PENINSULA** lies on the south west coast of Ireland by the Atlantic Ocean. The peninsula is especially beautiful when you look at its lovely beaches surrounded by steep rising cliffs and then topped off with the views of Mount Brandon which reaches 952 meters. The same named town of Dingle is a small harbour town with Ireland's least best kept secret. The most famous resident of Dingle and infamous in Ireland is 'Fungie' the Dingle Dolphin. Fungie has been visiting Dingle's shores since 1984 and many come there

Gallarus Oratory

to swim with him. In the north west part of the peninsula, there is the **GALLARUS ORATORY** which originates from the early Christian times of the eighth century. A special feature of this tiny architectural wonder is its sloped walls that make it so different from other buildings in the area.

📍 *Gallarus Oratory, Caherdorgan South, V92 Y028, Co. Kerry*
+353 66 915 5333, ↗ dingle-peninsula.ie

In the middle of the idyllic landscapes of Dingle, we find the **DINGLE DISTILLERY**. As with many Irish distilleries, this one retained the traditional practice of using three copper stills in the production of their blend. Also interesting is what this brewery does to really make its flavour and taste stand out from other products. To this day, they still bake the grains in a wood stove – a practice that's been discarded by most.

Warehouse (left), spirit safe, Dingle Whiskey Distillery, Dingle, Co. Kerry

Dingle Distillery Ltd. like many other distillery these days, produces both gin and vodka. The distillery is located in a converted sawmill in Milltown on the outskirts of Dingle. Dingle Distillery became the first independent Irish distillery to release a single pot still whiskey in several decades. The mild breeze from the sea really plays a role in the taste the whiskey later develops when the barrels are stored for the ageing process. Due to the small size of the distillery, only limited amounts are produced, but visitors can get a close up look of the distillation process and of course taste a bit of the final product.

♥ *Dingle Whiskey Distillery, V92 E7YD, Milltown, Dingle, Co. Kerry*
+353 86 777 5551, ↗ dingledistillery.ie

Crag Cave

A small detour along the N21 offers you a chance to see more of everyday Irish life, instead of the popular tourist places this book has descibed. Right before you get to Tralee, there is a well known system of caves called the **CRAG CAVE**, open to visitors. These caves are older than humanity itself and they show the power and beauty of nature. Long, long ago, water broke through the earth's crust and formed these wonderful caves.

The caves when discovered in 1983 were filled with water. As the water receded, new paths and tunnels were found showing many of the deposits and sediments left behind. Small water drops that formed on the walls and ceilings of the caves would later form the sharp stalagmites and stalactites that make the caves stand out as one of Ireland's most beautiful cave systems.

♥ *Crag Cave, Castleisland, V92 XK51, Co. Kerry,*
+353 66 714 1244, ↗ cragcave.com

Bally, Inch Beach, Co. Kerry

THE DINGLE-CORK TOUR

Many people from both Ireland and abroad claim that Co. Kerry is one on the most beautiful regions of the island. I can only partly agree with this, because Ireland, for me, offers something special in every part, due to its rich history and diverse traditions. That being said, Kerry really is a stunning corner of the country.

The three **PENINSULAS OF BEARA**, **DINGLE** and **IVERAGH** are surrounded by the Atlantic Ocean and have so many shades of green, they simply can't be named. Its old cloisters built from rocks older than time, really are very special. Even the streets here are different, with their narrow laneways, so small, that traffic can only go in one direction.

Throughout the whole region you can find lots of walking and cycle paths where you can get close to nature. On the peninsulas of Kerry and West Cork there are protected wildlife parks where bird watching and simple day strolls are a perfect way to spend your time. As this part of Ireland's landscape is more rugged, never having had much industrial or urban development, a lot of the historical buildings like the houses and castles have been left to decay. A sort of international friendship has blossomed out of this need to preserve these old buildings. So, due to the lack of upkeep of the older historical buildings, this area of Ireland almost seems to be locked in time, largely unchanged for centuries. I imagine this will be all the more charming for visitors.

As this area has a wide variety of things to visit, I will just give a small summary of the castles and manor houses that are worth seeing: Ballyheigue Castle, Bunbeg Fort, Gallarus Castle, Listowel Castle, Minard Castle, Muckross House, Ross Castle and Staigue Fort. In my opinion, all or any of these are definitely worth a trip, but there are many more around the area to see. Ireland truly is a great place to explore.

Shortly before Killarney on the beautiful Lough Leane, we found **WAYWARD SPIRITS**. This whiskey business was established with the name **HUNTING CAP WHISKEY**. The name reflects the spirit of the people of Kerry and of the O'Connell family in particular. From the base at Ballycarbery Castle, outside Cahirciveen, the family imported spirits and wines from Spain, France and the Netherlands. They supplied the gentry of Kerry from around 1475. After the castle was sacked by Cromwell's troops, they moved to Derrynane and there began a period of prosperity. The business built up under Maurice 'Hunting Cap' O'Connell becoming much larger. Although the imposition of excise duties made the business illegitimate, they were protected from the interference of the Revenue men of the

time by their geographical location – a natural harbour, invisible from the sea and surrounded by mountains controlled by the family. Their customers who did not want their supply of fine spirits interrupted, also played a part in this. The family moved to the Lakeview Estate in 1820 and built the current house in 1870. It was built in a stunning setting, overlooking a lake and mountains. Two hundred years later, the O'Connells have re-entered the *Hunting Cap Whiskey, Lakeview Estate, Killarney* family business and are working towards becoming a single estate 'Grain to Glass Distillery', with all the input coming from their own farm and the distilling done on site. This will take some time to achieve.

As I write, they are growing their first crop of barley, which later this year will be harvested and sent, together with water from the estate, to a contract distiller to be made into a pot still spirit, using their mash. This will be returned to the estate for maturation in their bonded warehouse. Although they do not produce their own spirits, they want to add their own touch, by finishing it on site in export barrels for 9–12 months until they feel it is ready to bottle and sell. In 2021, they hope to have the distillery fully operational and a visitor centre open. Until then, however, the site must remain private.

📍 *Hunting Cap Whiskey, Lakeview Estate, Killarney,*
+353 89 422 8836 ↗ huntingcapwhiskey.com

After ten minutes on the N72, you'll come to **KILLARNEY**. Killarney is not only well known for its **NATIONAL PARK** and **MUCKROSS HOUSE**, an old manor house, or **ROSS CASTLE**, the local castle, but also for the **'IRISH WHISKEY EXPERIENCE'** attraction. Here you have the opportunity to combine some of the local food, like farmers' cheese, or locally produced chocolate with some Irish whiskey. If you want to try your hand at making your own whiskey, they also offer a master class for all those 'wannabe' whiskey connoisseurs.

Overall, a trip to the 'Irish Whiskey Experience' is a welcome break for your senses and will allow you to become informed in the whiskey making process and further involved in the historical details surrounding the Irish whiskey industry. The selection

Celtic Whiskey Bar, 'Irish Whiskey Experience', Killarney

of master classes and learning opportunities is quite a large one, so here there really is a chance to gain insider's knowledge.

↗ celticwhiskeybar.com, ↗ irishwhiskeyexperience.net

If from Killarney you choose to visit the **RING OF KERRY** – a beautiful drive and well worth spending a full day or more – there is a chocolate factory where visitors are welcome. Here, you'll also find The Puffin Cafe, which opens from Easter until the end of September.

The setting is so spectacular with Skellig Michael in the background, that it was used as a location in the latest Star Wars movie 'The last Jedi'. You needn't fear though, it's highly unlikely that you'll run into Darth Vader.

📍 *Skellig's Chocolate Factory, St. Finians Bay, The Glen, Ballinskelligs V23 HP64, Co. Kerry, +35366 947 9119* ↗ skelligschocolate.com

The most direct way from Killarney to Cork is on the N71. The scenic drive along the N71 which cuts through the borders of east Cork and along the coast of south Cork is one of the many dreamy drives you can take from the west to head back to Cork city.

On the way, especially if like Shem, you're a bit of a chocoholic, you might consider visiting another chocolate maker. About 16 km from Kenmare, there's a shop and post office where a well-travelled award winning French chef, Benoit Lorge, has settled and produces unique chocolates in a French style which you can buy directly in his shop or even order online.

Lorge Chocolatier on the N71, Bonane, Kenmare, Co. Kerry

📍 *Lorge Chocolatier, Bonane, Kenmare, Co. Kerry, +353 64 66 79 994* ↗ lorge.ie

Co. Cork is the largest county in Ireland and for that reason it is split into parts like West and South Cork. West Cork has a mild ocean climate which to my mind, makes it one of the most ideal places in Ireland to be. For a city dweller like me, just getting to see the different colours of the roses, irises, and the never-ending fuchsia hedges were a treat.

This part of the island will leave you wanting more and more of such natural beauty.

If you keep driving on the N71, you will drive through Lambs Head Peninsula. Half of this belongs to Co. Cork and the other half to Co. Kerry. We will continue on our journey in the part that belongs to West Cork. No matter which peninsula you visit, do consider going to Mizen Head or Lambs Head, because as I just mentioned above, it really does not get any better than this in terms of undisturbed nature.

Lambs Head, West Cork

Due to the location of the peninsulas, the Gulf Stream flows along the coasts and allows all types of plants, even exotic ones that would usually only thrive in warm climates to grow. It's no wonder that on the Beara Peninsula, the Dzogchen Beara Meditation Centre found a home. It doesn't matter whether you are Buddhist or not, here accommodation is offered to anyone who is simply looking for relaxation and meandering paths to explore. It is an extremely popular destination and should be booked well in advance. The Peninsula remains almost as untouched as it was 30 or 40 years ago – wild and rugged with fantastic views of the mountains and sea. As a starting point I can't recommend this B&B enough. Check it out if you are going to visit the area.

📍 *B&B Dzogchen Beara, Garranes, Allihies, West Cork,*
+353 27 73 032 ↗dzogchenbeara.org

At the end of the Peninsula in Ballaghboy, you will encounter cable cars that bring you to the Island of Ballycrispin, where you can find many different walking trails. Not far from **GLENGARRIFF** and in the mountains, you'll find **BARLEY LAKE** with undisturbed views of the Atlantic Ocean. Before you visit, I recommend you save the coordinates of the lake, as it's not very easy to find.

↗glengarriff.ie

If you keep following the N71 you will come to **BALLYLICKEY** and then further on, switch to the R584 and follow it to lake **GOUGANE BARRA**. Besides the tranquil lake views, you will also find one of Ireland's

smallest churches. Together with the lake and views of the mountains nearby, this small and off-the-beaten-track church has become a popular wedding destination. Heading along the N71 in the direction of Ballyde-hob, you have a chance to take a delightful detour to **MIZEN PENINSULA** and the **MIZEN HEAD LIGHTHOUSE**. It's the most southwesterly lighthouse in Ireland. It has a

St. Finbarr's Oratory, Gougane Barra

visitor centre and if there's good weather, you can look out on to the Atlantic for as far as the eye can see.

Through **SKIBBEREEN**, you can take the N71 and switch onto the R595, which will bring you to the town of **BALTIMORE**. From the coastal town there are ferries to the islands of Cape Clear and Sherkin. Baltimore offers additional visiting options like its sailing centre and fishing harbour. If you want to visit some charming restaurants and pubs that you will like-ly remember long after you leave, then you have come to the right place. Trips to the **CAPE CLEAR ISLAND** and **SHERKIN ISLAND** are definitely

Beara Peninsula, West Cork Coast

worth taking too. Cape Clear puts a big importance on belonging to one of Ireland's Irish speaking communities or Gaeltacht. The is-landers are toying with the idea of opening up a whiskey distillery. Before anything can be set in stone, they must first solve the issue of getting fresh water to the planned distillery. If you are curious how this will pan out, you can follow the progress online. At the moment the **CAPE CLEAR DISTILLERY** (Comharchumann Cleire Teo) is still just an idea.

While in Baltimore, an outing to Sherkin Island only 10 minutes away, is another trip to check off the list. Sherkin Island is best known for its beautiful beaches and colourful village houses. Dive into the life of the island and don't forget that the best mussels in Ireland can be found at the **JOLLY ROGER PUB**.

Along the N71 lie many beautiful coastal towns like **GLANDORE**, **SCHULL**, **BALLYDE-HOB** and **SKIBBEREEN**, just to name a few. Each one of them offers places to go and enjoy fresh seafood, mostly caught on the same day! Castles, old roman ruins, forts, stone circles and lighthouses, coupled with the detailed history of smuggling and copper

Drombeg Stone Circle, Glandore - close to Skibbereen

mining, not to mention the mild weather of the gulf stream, make this an unforgettable part of the coastline. In addition, this beautiful area includes a number of hidden sandy beaches and enjoys a mild climate all year round due to the influence of the Gulf Stream. You may even come across a rare blue pearl, which, rumor has it, was part of a trove from the wreck of a Spanish pirate ship.

SKIBBEREEN is a tourist centre in the area as it is on the way to places like **MIZEN PENINSULA**. The town is well known for its arts and crafts produced by locals, as well as the many 'blow-ins' – i.e. those who come, fall in love with the place and stay soon becoming locals too – and as in any part of this area, there are always new restaurants and cosy pubs to explore. A short distance away is **LOUGH HYNE**, an undisturbed saltwater lake in the middle of a forest. Lough Hyne is ideal for swimming, snorkeling or even canoeing.

St Patrick's Cathedral, Skibbereen

Skibbereen has one of the newer distilleries in Co. Cork – the **WEST CORK DISTILLERS**. In 2003, three friends came up with the idea of opening a distillery and since 2008, have specialised in making alcoholic drinks. Local spring water is used for the production of the spirits and thanks to the mild climate that surrounds the area, it gives the drinks a memorable flavour.

A special thing about this brewery is that all the machines used in the production of its spirits were made and built by craft workers in Skibbereen. Now that's what you call real craftsmanship. As in most small breweries, not only is whiskey produced, but vodka, gin and poitín too. Their whiskey assortments include Blended: Bourbon Cask, Intense Cask and Black Cask and Single Malt: 10 and 12 Years Old.

The brewery, at this time, is in the middle of relocating to bigger warehouses and later in 2018 they will have a visitor centre. The hall being used at the moment will later become a storehouse. What exactly you will find and discover might still be unknown, but you won't have to worry about the quality or availability of whiskey and the beautiful landscapes on offer.

📍 *West Cork Distillers, Marsh Road, Skibbereen, P81 YY31 West Cork, +353 28 22 815,* ↗ **westcorkdistillers.com**

About 30 minutes away from Cork is the small town of Clonakilty, located in Clonakilty Bay. Here you will find one of the other new distilling ventures of Cork, the **CLONAKILTY DISTILLERY**. It's owned by the Scully family and their special goal is to produce their whiskey from different varieties of barley. The distillery lies in the heart of Clonakilty and the warehouse is on the Galley Head, not far from the lighthouse. The climate here on the Atlantic, with mists coming in from the sea, make it the perfect place for the production and storage of whiskey. The spring water that is used in the distillation process goes through a natural filtering system as it runs through sandstone and barite. Following in

Clonakilty Distillery

the traditional style, the whiskey is distilled in three copper stills. The Scully family are planning to introduce a pot still whiskey to their collection along with a new variety of gin. On the tour you can admire the three pot stills and the pot still for the gin production.

Clonakilty Distillery, Visitors Centre

In special gin courses offered, you can even distill your own gin.

📍 *Clonakilty Distillery, The Waterfront, Clonakilty, P85 K720, West Cork, 51 37' 17.21 N, 8 53' 10.37 W, +353 23 884 0635*

↗ **clonakiltydistillery.ie**

Continuing along the N71 in the direction of Cork, you could stop off in the small coastal town of **KINSALE**, which you can reach by turning onto the R607. Hugely popular for sailing, the small colourful town offers many opportunities to cosy up in one of its numerous small pubs or to try some of its excellent food. Some call Kinsale the 'Gourmet Capital

Kinsale Town

of Ireland'. If you are looking to sample some first-class dining experiences, you won't have a problem with that here. Other than that, Kinsale, which has a strong Spanish influence due to the invasion in 1601, still holds some of the old charm that only old cities and towns possess. Kinsale was built in the form of a star shaped fort and is, to this day, one of the most visited places on the south coast of Ireland. You will not be short of ideas for things to do here and can enjoy a variety of activities like sailing and golf. One thing is for sure, once people visit they always come back.

Here our trip must come to an end, but that doesn't mean that you have to stop tasting! I hope you had at least half as much fun as Shem and I and that you also had an enjoyable, informative, but not too 'tipsy' experience while reading Ireland's Whiskey Guide. Perhaps the book will motivate you to come to Ireland and experience the history, landscape, little treasures and unique art of Irish whiskey making throughout the island of Ireland.

Sláinte!

Acknowledgments

Someone wrote: "having an idea and turning it into a book is as hard as it sounds." I could not express that better. This is why I want to thank EVERYONE who ever said anything positive to me or taught me something. I heard it all, I listened and it meant something.

A very special thanks go to my father who taught me that "I can do whatever I want but I have to get up and start walking and if I start something I should also bring it to an end." I thank him for that, even though he is no longer with us. His words have accompanied me through the whole project. I also want to thank him for giving me the love of photography, without which this book would only be half as beautiful.

I especially want to thank the individuals that helped make this book happen. Complete thanks to Keith McDonnell (Irish Whiskey Museum), Bernard and Rosemary Walsh and their Relationship Manager Woody Kane (Royal Oak Distillery), Sean Braun (Donegal Castle), Stephen Teeling (Teeling Whiskey Distillery), Deirdre Keon (Midlands Whiskey Experiences), Moira and James Doherty (Sliabh Liag Distillery), Louise Mc Guane (J.J. Corry Irish Whiskey), Lynn and Shane Braniff (The Echlinville Distillery), Ally Alpine (Irish Whiskey Experience and Celtic Whiskey Bar & Larder), Gerry Ginty (Powerscourt Distillery), Kilbeggan Distillery Experience Centre (the unknown tour guide who started in me the love for Irish whiskey), Ursula Barry (Jameson Distillery Midleton), Trevor Williams Archivist from Bushmills Whiskey Distillery, Aileen Eglington (AE Consulting), Aideen Gohery (Critical Digital), Sean O'Neil (singer and songwriter), Jackie Leahy, Delisha Duran, Tino Ehrhardt, Sophie Morgner, Robert Fliegel, Seamus Tobin, Clár Ní Bhuachalla, Trish Tobin, Ingrid Jungmann, Jana.

… and everyone that I met on the way and that got me on the right path – unfortunately I do not know all the names and for reasons of space, I cannot mention them. I thank you all.